"In *Learning from My Father* David Johnson shares with all of us a unique gift he received from his own father. His eight lessons touch on challenges all believers face, and his compelling dialogue with his father, along with his own life story, shines a bright light on what it means to be Christian and how we as Christians must understand our calling."

— **JOHN C. LECHLEITER**
Chairman, President, and CEO,
Eli Lilly and Company

"In writing this marvelous tribute to his father, David Johnson has also given us a gift. This little book imparts much wisdom and inspiration!"

— **RICHARD J. MOUW**
President, Fuller
Theological Seminary

"In this beautifully written memoir David Lawther Johnson reveals not only profound lessons he learned from his father but also deep wisdom for all of us about living courageous and faithful lives. To read this book is to reflect about what truly matters in our closest relationships and in the ways we number our days."

— **THOMAS G. LONG**
Emory University

D0096894

"Parent and child interacting profoundly in life and death. A familial faith journey captured in precious letters back and forth. Questions of faith become doorways to grace as told in this marvelous exchange between parent and child. Grace passed from one generation to the next may, in fact, be the greatest gift."

— DANIEL F. EVANS
President and CEO,
Indiana University Health

"In this rare and wonderful book Johnson invites all of us to think deeply about what it means to live the Christian life. Read it alone and be enriched. Read it with others and let it deepen your conversations. Read it with your young adult daughters and sons and begin a correspondence of your own. This is a very special book by an unusually thoughtful Christian layperson and a dear friend."

— CRAIG DYKSTRA
Senior Vice President, Religion,
Lilly Endowment Inc.

LEARNING FROM MY FATHER

Lessons on Life and Faith

David Lawther Johnson

William B. Eerdmans Publishing Company

Grand Rapids, Michigan / Cambridge, U.K.

Published 2012 by
Wm. B. Eerdmans Publishing Co.
2140 Oak Industrial Drive N.E., Grand Rapids, Michigan 49505 /
P.O. Box 163, Cambridge CB3 9PU U.K.

Printed in the United States of America

18 17 16 15 14 13 12   7 6 5 4 3 2 1

Library of Congress Cataloging-in-Publication Data

Johnson, David Lawther.
Learning from my father: lessons on life and faith / David Lawther Johnson.
        p.   cm.
ISBN 978-0-8028-6708-7 (pbk.: alk. paper)
1. Christian life.   I. Title.

BV4501.3.J63275   2012
248.4 — dc23

2011045359

www.eerdmans.com

For his (and my) loving and beloved family —
Anne Johnson, Jerry Johnson Jr.,
Anne Nobles, and Catherine Nobles Johnson —
and my constant friend and loving father of lifelong lessons,
the Reverend Gerald R. Johnson, D.D.

Contents

vii

Contents

THE LAST LESSON

His last lesson in life was how to leave it.

In this as in all else, I was his student. I thought we'd have three months. That was the estimate his doctor gave me, on a rushed 7 A.M. cell-phone call to announce the suddenly discovered, incurable gallbladder cancer in early spring 2004. That was the time I began to count, and count on. I was scrambling, but at least, being with him was something I could do. I wanted to do it "right." He was in no pain, and under minimal medication. His mind was clear, even if his body had betrayed him. And so I wanted to have chances to reflect with this man — my lifelong friend and teacher — on what it all meant, how he felt, the state of his health and the state of his faith in medicine, family, and, most importantly, God. But as it turned out, we had less than three weeks. And then he was gone.

He knew he was going, long before I did. After all, he was a pastor by vocation, having spent a career of nearly fifty years in hospitals, nursing homes, and hospices ministering to the sick and the dying. During his own admission and preliminary tests at the hospital, he studied the concerned expressions of the medical residents examining him, and quickly confirmed the hopelessness of his condition. The doctor then arrived, reviewed the charts, and made the bad news official. The patient was uncharacteristically withdrawn for about two hours, clearly desiring to be left alone. When we rejoined him, he was sobered and sad. Even at this tough moment, however, he declared himself ready for whatever came next.

What came immediately next was yet another exhausting change of setting, with a move from hospital to hospice. Finally allowed to rest more comfortably in quieter surroundings, he began to get busy. He made it clear he had people to see, and good-byes to say. True to his intellect and his integrity, he didn't try to hide the fact that he was not ready to die, and that he believed there to be considerable portions of the world and its people still needing him to put things right. Advice and opinions flowed ever more freely. He even began, rather joyously, to abandon a lifetime's worth of those political skills that are the hallmark of a good pastor — familiar traditions like seeing all comers without hesitation or distinction, expressing and sharing concerns for all, or dispensing advice and good humor to everyone. Now, knowing his time was short, he determined to speak only with those he really cared to see. For the rest, he feigned sleep or confusion. How wonderful it was one morning to watch a pious, pompous fellow clergyman come to his side, hoping for a final and quotable conversation, only to find the afflicted with his eyes stubbornly shut and his breathing heavy. As the unfulfilled pilgrim tiptoed away, the dying man's eyes flickered to become slits, and then fully opened. And then, to me — his son — my father winked.

The next several days, before the onslaught of painkillers in overwhelming doses, were his best. He spent many hours with our then eleven-year-old daughter, with whom he had always had a special, easy relationship and who, like my mother, was now determined never to leave his side. He spoke warmly as a parent with my brother Jerry, who now commuted back and forth from his home in Michigan, bringing both stability and strength to all of us. And he spoke fondly, like a parent, with my wife Anne, whom he had always loved as a daughter, and who continued to supply him with favorite books and favorite food for as long as he could maintain an appetite for either one.

Then usually, toward the end of a long day of tests and conversations, he would turn his attention to me. He was ready to talk. We would discuss the sorry state of world affairs, the sorrier state of domestic politics, the stories of those who had come to see him, and most importantly, how he was holding up. Throughout, he remained fully engaged, neither wistful nor sentimental. He was sad but never visibly scared. He spoke of being "on a new journey," but did not dwell on his emotions surrounding it. From his substantial library assembled over a lifetime, he requested only T. S. Eliot's small volume *The Four Quartets* — fittingly, first published in the United States in 1943, the year of his ordination to the ministry. He focused on certain verses, especially the affirmation of *East Coker* that "In my end is my beginning," and the observation in *The Dry Salvages* that "These are only hints and guesses, / Hints followed by guesses; and the rest / Is prayer, observance, discipline, thought and action." (He concluded that he'd done pretty well in at least four out of those five categories, coming up short only in his demonstrated powers of productive prayer.)

Time accelerated, as my father declined. He slept far more. When he was awake, his attitude was positive. At times he seemed almost excited as to what awaited him next. The final time we spoke, before he lapsed into one last deep sleep, my father asked for my views on a number of subjects, secular and religious. Happily for me, he appeared generally satisfied with my responses. His final advice was to indulge in my — to me, still hidden — sense of humor. He also suggested I might occasionally offer a few lighter notes of evidence of enjoying life more.

His calling and funeral (drawing upon years of pastoral preparations, he had planned the service, down to the hymns, long before) brought out hundreds from all walks of life. Former church members and fellow clergy, of course, as well as community leaders, neighbors, fellow residents from the retirement center — all were there. But there too were the waitresses from favorite restaurants he had counseled over the years, the bank clerks he had befriended, the janitors he had slipped an occasional five-dollar bill to over time, the middle-aged businessmen from the local restaurant who had delighted in seeing him for coffee many mornings and arguing over issues of "God and country" (my father was equally adept at voicing provocative views on both). His touch had extended in all directions, blind to distinctions of age, occupation, or social standing.

This was his life, and this was the quality of his faith. Like the crowd that came to his calling, his presence was diversely rich. He touched people where they lived and as they lived, without platitudes or contrivance. His message was almost always action-focused. He could be counted upon to respond sharply to unloving or bigoted conduct, without coming across as judgmental. And as I saw in my last hours alone with him, his was a faith that started and stayed real — certain and sure, stubbornly unsentimental.

That faith was the work of a lifetime for my father, Gerald R. Johnson. Typical of many in his "Greatest Generation," he was a child of immigrants, in his case Danish, people who left the cold and rocky soil of Scandinavia with high hopes for a new land and a new life in America, only to find themselves (remarkably, without irony) settling in exactly the same type of bankrupt terrain they thought they had left behind: deep into the frigid upper peninsula of Michigan. My grandfather ended up as a section worker for one of the railroads that carried ore and timber across the landscape of this bleak territory. My grandmother raised her children, supervised a large nearby contingent of resettled relatives from home, took in boarders, and prepared meals of homegrown food. My father once observed that there was only one advantage in being as poor as his family was: when the markets fell as the Great Depression of 1929 arrived, no one much noticed — because his family had never been part of the market economy in the first place.

My grandmother knew that education in America could bring an end to the cycles of poverty that marked her family's only true legacy. Early on, my father, as the "caboose" of his siblings and demonstrably the most intellectually curious, was singled out as the one who might ascend into acceptable American society. In the community of Escanaba, Michigan, where he grew up, only one family had (or, arguably, needed) anyone who had achieved a college education: the local clergyman, who superintended a Presbyterian congregation and had a son my father's age. Accordingly, my father was encouraged to follow his classmate's lead. When the boy finished high school, so did my father — the first member of his family, in fact, to advance beyond the fifth grade. When his friend gained admission to Alma College, a small Presbyterian-based school in Michigan's lower peninsula, my father did so as well. And when his friend decided to move to a larger and more cosmopolitan (though still Presbyterian) environment by transferring to the College of Wooster in northern Ohio, my father followed. The fact that his friend Peter was a Presbyterian, or might believe in some particular form of religious teachings, was of no particular consequence to my father. In truth, religion had played no role in his upbringing; my father was fully fifteen years old before he even set foot inside a church. The wonderful biblical stories of Noah, Jonah, arks, floods, loaves, and fishes were all unknown and consequently irrelevant to him. Instead, what mattered was that his best friend was leaving home, sidestepping poverty, and going somewhere. My father determined to do likewise. And thus, when Peter took the ultimate career step of entering Princeton Theological Seminary, Jerry Johnson managed to find his way there too.

At Princeton, my father finally came into his own. He learned the stories and lessons of the Old Testament and the

New — for the first time. Also for the first time, as he later told me, he came to feel fully aware. Lacking any exposure to religious thinking in his upbringing, my father had scant need to reconcile a child's faith with an adult's knowledge. In his case, learning had center stage all to itself; faith was an intellectually coherent way of living that flowed from that learning process, rather than challenging it. It all came together for him, there and then: Jerry Johnson graduated first in his seminary class, winning top honors in preaching.

Following graduation, my father progressed through a succession of churches — first in rural Ohio, later in a larger urban congregation in Toledo, and eventually in a significant posting as the senior pastor of an even larger Presbyterian church in Indianapolis. He "retired" from that church in his early sixties, only to find himself immersed well into his late seventies in a series of calls as interim pastor for several congregations across the United States. These opportunities arose as each church worked through the seemingly endless cycle of candidate committee and task-force meetings in which the Presbyterian denomination excels as churches select new pastoral leadership. (In his highly readable 1965 book *The Revolution of the Saints: A Study in the Origin of Radical Politics,* analyzing the historical intertwining of politics and the Calvinist following upon which Presbyterianism is based, the political scientist Michael Walzer observed of John Calvin, "There have been few men in history who loved meetings more.")

Throughout, my father's intellectual curiosity remained strong, and his talents proved considerable. More than anything else, he was simply grateful. He once confessed that he had met most of his ambitions just by leaving home and getting an education; everything that followed was a bonus.

Yet there is more to his story than that. Somehow along the way, even though — or perhaps because — he came to the subject of faith with truly a blank slate, my father also became a believer in the message of the gospel. He was a steady adherent to the concept that life on earth was not an end in itself, but rather a part and a piece of God's larger plan for the eternal life of his creation, a plan in which people played a significant role through what he always saw as the "relationship of faith." I'm sure that relationship was never easy for him, as it is challenging for us all. Yet this was no gloomy Calvinist, even though he was highly attuned to the frailties of the world and its people. Instead, he was an essential optimist with a spare, solid, but hopeful approach to belief. He frequently questioned the shape of God's plans for the world; he never really doubted God's grace.

This was the man I knew to the end — one who was not changed by life's ending. And that was his last lesson to me, shown rather than said: make sure you develop a type of rugged faith, a religious belief you hold credible and true, because you never know when that faith will need to withstand the limits of life itself. Don't waste time indulging in easy or sentimental, overemotional expressions of religious conviction when those sentiments are bound to fail as you barely have the energy to breathe, and all you can count on is who you are, and those (ideally, including God himself) who love you for that.

It was great teaching, a fitting, final lesson in life and faith.

It was not, however, his only guidance for me. My father

had blessed me with important lessons earlier in my life as well, as I came to recall a few weeks after his death. These arose from a correspondence between us at the time I began college, almost forty years earlier. As a freshman at Harvard University, I had found myself with many predictable questions about life and belief. Like my father's journey east to Princeton Seminary a generation earlier, I was suddenly far away from my Midwestern home, on the "big stage" of a legendary American university for the first time, insecure and very much exposed to a staggering array of sophisticated new people, words and thoughts, academic ideals (and academic cynicism too). All at once I was unsure of many things. I had always been close to both of my parents, and still spoke with them often by telephone. Yet the subject of religion, to me, somehow called for a more structured discussion. Hence, on matters of faith, I usually wrote to my father and hoped for his responsive counsel by return mail.

I was not disappointed. My father readily embraced this opportunity to open what he clearly felt to be a long-overdue discussion. He wrote back, and kept writing — as did I. At the time, the resulting correspondence achieved its desired effect. I eagerly read what he had to say on the subjects of God, Christ, Christianity, faith, and good and evil, and found his words to be both affirming and helpful. Fortunately, despite many moves over many ensuing years, I managed to save our "honest exchange" of letters and thoughts on those several topics of faith I had implored him to address.

I hadn't thought about those letters, however, for a long time. In fact, it was not until I found myself, at my mother's insistence, as the new custodian of my late father's many books and papers (along with his desk, bookcases, church photographs, and virtually all the other contents of his study) that I recalled this particular correspondence. Joyous in my rediscovery, I saw anew how much my father had said — and in a real sense, still had to say — about life and faith.

Much has changed, of course, since we wrote to one another in the early 1970s. In rereading these letters, I was sobered by the realization that I was now older than my father had been when we began this correspondence. Now too, I had my own life experiences to compare to his, and my own encounters with faith to recall and compare to the perspective he provided as I was emerging into adulthood. And now I also had my own child, clearly determined to continue our family tradition of entering college far away from home.

Initially, I determined to take this material and write my father's biography, showing how he had developed an inspirational but highly workable faith in a way that allowed him to deal with life fully and to face death squarely. As I thought more about it, however, I realized my father might actually prefer an active demonstration of his legacy over a more passive recounting of his life. His letters to me on religious faith were the foundation of that legacy, but even more, he had wanted his words to be a foundation for my actions. "It's always important to be clear what we're talking about," he wrote in one of those letters. "And if we're talking about your faith, what that really means is we're talking about your being faithful: how well you have conscientiously, steadfastly tried to pattern your life after what you have accepted from and seen in the teacher." Well, he was certainly my teacher. So how well had I heard what that teacher was saying? How credible — and now, how teachable to my own daughter — were the beliefs he described to me?

Perhaps not quite yet "old," but certainly well beyond the years of questioning youth, I should be able to address directly, and now in the context of my own experience, the major issues my father and I struggled over in that correspondence so long ago. They remain the basic issues of my life, because they are the basic themes that concern us all: belief, love, faith, sin, evil, death, and hope.

He offered a seasoned and sensible framework to consider each. Taken together, my father's letters formed what became for me — at a critical time, and over time — an essential Christian lesson plan. Did I learn it? Have I followed through on what he taught? What do these words have to say right now to my life, and to the lives of others? And if these lessons really do still work for me, what am I doing to pass them on? Certainly, mine are no longer questions that must await some passage of many years for answers. Almost four decades later, it seems high time to give my father's lessons another visit.

The First Lesson

BEGINNING WITH BELIEF

E arly on in my life, when it came to religion, there was an open question whether I would turn out to be a believer or a renegade.

In many respects, I'm a natural "believer" candidate. Now fifty-eight years old, I am the son, the grandson, and the great-grandson of Presbyterian pastors — a lineage spanning both my paternal and maternal lines. My mother's father had a faith strong enough to sustain him as a chaplain ministering to the dead and dying in the trenches of France at the end of World War I. I had one great-uncle who was a fine pastor and a fair preacher, even though he could not hear; I had another great-uncle who, a century ago, decided to leave his practice as a Midwestern physician and sign on as a medical missionary in South Africa. Presbyterian colleges, seminaries, and churches have abounded on the landscapes of those coming before me.

In other ways, though, I'm also a pretty good prospect for

renegade status when it comes to traditional, organized religion, because I've seen so much of it. I know many children of pastors (known as "PKs," or preachers' kids) who, as adults, profess to want nothing whatsoever to do with churches, creeds, or theology. PK status is an interesting but often intense way to grow up, in a household where ideas are meant to be vigorously debated, and as part of a family that is generally on display every Sunday morning and often throughout the week at church events (including those always dreadful Wednesday evening pitch-in dinners) to parishioners ever on the lookout for "fallen angels." Preachers' kids get an unfiltered inside view of people, good and bad, and their attempts to organize (or at least justify) the shape of their lives and their beliefs in front of others. Cynicism is a constant risk. In comparing notes in later years, the contemporaries with whom I seem to have the most in common are the sons and daughters of politicians. Like PKs, some of these progeny have been captured by family traditions and migrated toward their own runs for public office. Many more of them, however, have fled as far away from politics as they can get.

In my case, by my late teens I had pretty much concluded that I did not want to "follow my father's footsteps" (this was often the way the question was phrased to me, usually with a patronizing chuckle, by members of our congregation) and continue the family legacy of a church-based vocation. Again the political references here are pertinent, since running a large church congregation requires an outsized portion of insight into human conduct and a very active, usually hidden mastery of the techniques of persuasion. The pastor is supposed to be the inspired mentor and inspirational facilitator.

Often, he or she also has to be the field marshal, the deal-maker or "business developer" seeking to hold a church together, to expand a congregation's size, or to finance new church facilities. My father was extremely good at all these things. Yet, so much of what he did seemed to go deliberately unrecognized, and definitely unrewarded, by those he was serving. I'm not sure if my ambitions were greater, but I knew from an early age that my ego was simply needier when it came to receiving validation.

I opted for another path — or at least, I assumed I had. My parents had taught me that there were four "true" professions: teaching, medicine, the law, and the ministry. Hesitant when it came to dealing with diseases or large volumes of blood, impatient with the "ivory tower" of academia, and reconciled to becoming the first male in my line in nearly a century to sidestep the clergy (even my older brother had enrolled in seminary for one exploratory semester), I opted for law.

My path was not direct. In truth, I didn't really want it to be, since I wasn't quite clear what a lawyer actually did, beyond working hard. So I continued to try to set something of my own course, though hardly an unconventional one. After college, I ended up studying history at Oxford, going back to Harvard for law school, and then working for a while on Capitol Hill as a staff member for the United States Senate Foreign Relations Committee. My four years there took me far afield, assessing and reporting back to committee members on the levels of effectiveness and integrity of U.S. foreign assistance and food-for-peace programs in places like Kenya, Tanzania, Uganda, Ivory Coast, and Zaire (subsequently renamed

Democratic Republic of the Congo). This was an ideal job for someone young and single, with an unrequited yearning for adventure and lacking significant responsibilities.

Eventually, though, the same sober side of my being that took me to law school in the first place began to point out, with mounting intensity, that I was likely to find few practical applications for my law degree in sub-Saharan Africa. I had worked hard for three, mostly miserable, years to earn the right to be called a lawyer; and now, the logic went, I needed to exercise that franchise. Staying in Washington would probably have meant becoming a lobbyist, an interesting and worthwhile pursuit in its own right, but not the way I thought I wished to practice law. Instead, I became convinced (and received good advice from others) that I belonged in a smaller, more manageable setting, someplace where a good business lawyer could have a direct impact on important transactions and, perhaps, do some significant good for the community as well. I had recently married (another lawyer), and my new spouse was wonderfully open to new challenges. Thus, life eventually returned me to Indianapolis and the practice of business law in a large corporate firm.

This return also served to nurture in me, for a very long period, an avocation for elective politics that I earnestly convinced myself was simply waiting to blossom, at the right time, as my life's ultimate calling. Thus for the moment, apart from the occasional political prayer breakfast or infrequent visit (usually, a bit late) to a back pew on Sunday morning, I found my most customary and comfortable company well outside the walls of the church.

But I never stopped wanting to believe in something.

Why is this so? Very early in life, I suppose I wanted to believe in the same way that I wanted to walk, or needed love — belief in its purest sense is a natural, human yearning, and a magnet for our most basic intellectual and emotional energies. That is why, I think, we come to our first beliefs through those we love, or respect, or both in our earliest days. Belief in virtually anything, even matters far smaller than the existence of God or the resurrection of Christ, remains a mere construct, without warmth or resonance unless imparted to us by someone we know and trust.

My father made this point to me in one of our earliest letters, using an example from his own childhood.

I think back, and it seems to me that this is the way I first learned how to multiply numbers in arithmetic. I had an authority, one of my early, favorite teachers; and you will recall that a teacher is a pretty big authority to a child. The teacher said that five times two is ten, and I took the word of the teacher as a fact. Perhaps I didn't really *know* that five times two is ten, but when I tested that fact against reality, it worked. I counted five fingers on each hand and I arrived at ten. And then I tested it out really seriously. I remember this very well because my cousin and I decided we would each buy a celluloid monkey on the end of a stick. It cost ten cents. My cousin had ten pennies and I had two nickels. I knew that his ten pennies would do it, but would my two nickels do the same? Do you remember that ten pennies always seemed like more money than two nickels or a dime when you were young?

This was a serious test — a real commitment, so to speak. And when I got the same celluloid monkey for two nickels that my cousin got for ten pennies, I *knew* the truth.

He quickly proceeded to his larger point:

Isn't that the way you and I ought to approach our religious beliefs? We find a person (or a group of persons) in whom we can believe — someone whose life is full, whose human relationships are rich, who seems to have mastered the secret of authentic humanity. A person, in other words, who is an authority. Emotion is not the key to this kind of personal authority. And intellect or erudition is not the secret either. You don't look for an authority in a person who is, as John Milton says, "deeply vers'd in books, and shallow in himself." It must be someone whose own life shows that he knows what life is all about. Now we don't *know* that that person's beliefs are true for us. But we test what he tells us is true against reality to see if it works. And, most importantly, we test those beliefs seriously, desperately, and with commitment.

And then he brought the lesson home by recalling a time when, as a physically awkward young child, I was terrified of water (and pretty much everything else) and thus convinced I could never learn to swim.

Do you remember how we went to the lake every summer when you were little? And everyone went swimming — your cousins, your aunts and uncles, your brother

Jerry, and Mother and I — everyone, that is, but you. You sat on a rock in about two inches of water, and you cried every time a wave got you a bit wet. You were about five then. You wanted to swim, but you were afraid. I used to say to you, "Dave, anyone can swim. All you have to do is to get out into the water and move your arms and legs the way I show you, and the water will hold you up." You said you believed me; but you didn't really believe me because you did not try to swim. Then one morning toward the end of the summer you announced at the breakfast table, "Today I'm going to swim." I don't think your mother and Jerry and I really believed you. But when breakfast was over, you marched resolutely down to the dock, right out to the very end of it, and jumped off into the water. I remember I came running after you to pull you out; but you managed all by yourself. You struggled and splashed around and you made it to the shore. And that day you did learn to swim. It was then you really believed that the water would hold you up. The authority was a help. He was the beginning. What he taught you was a help. But it wasn't until you took him seriously and tried it that you really learned to swim. This is what the Danish scholar Søren Kierkegaard means when he calls faith a "leap." You took a real Kierkegaardian leap that day. And your faith became knowledge — you knew and you could swim.

My father concluded his story with a further effort to root me firmly in the community of believers, observing that I would never have had the courage (or the craziness) to jump into unseen waters had I simply read an instruction manual on how to swim: "You were willing to try it because I told you that you could do it. There was this deeply personal angle involved, a loving and concerned authority that seemed to make the whole thing possible and reasonable."

Clearly, I was fortunate to have someone I trusted there from the start, someone who could impart to me an approach to pretty much everything, including religion and faith, in a way that made sense to me. This occurred not because my father was a professional expert on these topics (though indeed he was) but simply because he was my father, and seemed to be in good control of his own life as well as mine. Most people I know who describe themselves as religious believers have come to (or stayed with) their convictions not because of a single moment, or by a sudden conversion, but through a long-developed relationship with a parent, a friend, or a spouse who was himself or herself simply believable and thus made belief seem sensible and right. Certainly, that is how I explain myself, and how I have gotten here.

I often wonder why adherents to more dramatic forms of evangelism are not better attuned to this basic human truth. Fiery sermons from pastors, fervent testimonials from strangers, door-to-door solicitations from earnest young converts — these may all speak impressively to the passion that burns in the heart of some believers. But they are likely to fall far short of making a lasting difference in the lives of those who encounter them, or hear them, because there is no underlying relationship to make their message compelling. It is not that the message is necessarily wrong, or weak, or insufficient; it's that the messenger does not have standing to offer it to someone he or she does not truly know. Even to a child, Christianity cannot be force-fed.

So it helps when belief starts credibly and close to home, as it did for me. But belief also has to continue to make a difference to each of us — a personal, important difference that we don't just hang on to but stay with and build upon because it is somehow useful. In my case, reliance upon the image of a created, compassionate universe, where individuals and individual actions might actually matter, continued to make sense even as I got older and the choices got harder. Such belief helped me make decisions when I needed that help. It provided me with a basic safety net for figuring out where I was, and what I should be doing next.

Never was this more apparent for me than in the depressing days following what was probably my inevitable, and spectacularly unsuccessful, run for public office. As noted earlier, throughout those college years when I was writing to my father, subsequently as a graduate student and law student, then as a young staff worker on Capitol Hill, and later still as a politically active (and no longer so young) lawyer building a practice that connected me frequently to community and political leaders, I maintained a basic conviction that someday I would cross the line from earnest apprentice and perennial campaign adviser to full-fledged political candidate. In retrospect, I should have been more attentive to the observation made years earlier by my wife Anne: that most people claiming such a passion for politics "certainly moved a lot faster" toward that life than I appeared to be doing. Indeed, single-minded focus bordering on zeal may well be the most essential attribute for success in any aspiring politician. Mine was just a more gentlemanly, less intense, but still strong ambition, I assured her — and myself. There would be a right time, and when it came, I would act.

In 2000, after my "preparatory period" of some seventeen years of legal practice, I finally did. Indiana's governor at that time was a good friend of mine (rarely in politics can such a statement actually be true, but in my case it was). I had played a significant advisory role in the governor's 1996 election and had also advised him on a range of policy and political issues in the following years. As he contemplated his own pending reelection effort, the governor grew concerned because no one he knew and trusted had stepped forward to join the ticket with him and run for the United States Senate seat that would also be contested that year; it was held by a four-term incumbent known and loved by all, someone who had never faced a remotely close election contest over nearly a quarter of a century. Volunteers for this sacrificial altar were understandably few. I became convinced that now indeed could be my moment. I reasoned (or perhaps more accurately, rationalized) that even though I would almost certainly fail in a contest where I began as a complete political unknown and was outmatched in almost every respect, I would not be outworked. I could therefore earn my way into serious contention for future races where I should be far more competitive. This was it, I convinced myself.

Of course, it wasn't. All those better-known candidates who decided to sit out this particular "opportunity" (as well as my father himself, who just said I was crazy even to attempt it) proved to be sage beyond their years. My little launch boat into electoral politics was rapidly overwhelmed, sinking deep into the tide of incumbent strength. On election night, of all of Indiana's ninety-two counties, I carried only one, failing to garner even a third of the statewide votes when all were finally counted.

Though I had known I would lose, defeat when it came was devastating — and simply, but truly, embarrassing. There were many moments when I had actually enjoyed being a candidate, even though hopelessly outmatched from the start. I found it stimulating to assemble a young and eager staff; surprisingly easy to ask total strangers for campaign funds; immensely satisfying to speak with voters about issues close to their hearts; strangely energizing to show up at plant gates to shake factory workers' hands during 4:30 A.M. shift changes; and most of all, reaffirming to emerge from the shadows, standing no longer as the adviser next to the candidate, but out front as the candidate himself. Donors were often generous to my long-shot campaign, and the media, though appropriately skeptical, were generally restrained in their criticism of my sanity. In a strange way, I had felt so firmly that politics was my calling that I became half convinced that, by some miracle, I might succeed — or at least come close. Perhaps more simply, I had grown so caught up in the intense process of running that the last thing on my mind, or in my heart, was to get myself prepared for the inevitability of defeat.

But defeat hit home — hard. And once that day was over, I drifted for weeks, occasionally making halfhearted and largely futile attempts to return to my legal practice. I became convinced that I had monumentally failed my family and friends, and came close to real despair when I tried to consider what to do with the rest of my life.

Here is where the framework of my father's faith took on new meaning for me. While I didn't recall these exact words at the time, my father's conviction that God's love tells us we are worth something, that we are known and cared about as individuals and that our actions matter, had stuck with me. That conviction was beautifully expressed to me long ago in one of our early letters:

We just don't believe in a God who hides behind the ramparts of heaven. This is not a casual God who enquires from time to time, in an offhand manner, about how we are getting along. I think it's a God who is one with us, all the way. This is a God willing to share our common human lot; one who understands fully our sin and sorrow and suffering. He knows the hopes, the ideals, the victories, the defeats; the trials and triumphs, the tears and tribulations of his human children. In a word, he understands. Understanding is what makes for a good marriage, a noble friendship, a fine relationship between doctor and patient, or pastor and people. In a time of crisis or need, it is understanding we seek — someone who knows and understands what we are going through.

That's how God loves us. He knows what we are really like. He knows the secret recesses of every human heart. He knows the things in us that we could not say to another living soul. He knows all these things — and he loves us in spite of them all.

Believing that somehow, despite the scale of the cosmos and the tiny footprint of my own life, I am known and appreciated by God in ways I cannot hope to understand, is profoundly reassuring. Perhaps even more important, such belief made me take my life and what I was doing about it more seriously. Time has always mattered, actions have always mattered, because somehow, in some way, I and everyone else here apparently matter and have some real, if modest, role in a created universe.

At this low moment of my own life, I was now wrestling — pretty fiercely — with what on earth my own particular role might actually be. What eventually came to me was hardly a flashing insight or some sudden moment of religious realization. It was just a feeling. A feeling that was far more basic, low, and rumbling, faint at first, but still familiar and somewhat comforting. Mounting over time, that feeling grew to be recognizable as a conviction of my own: defeated or not, disoriented or not, I was still someone with something to do, with a part to play in life, and I had better get back up on my feet and get on with it.

I began to take stock. I asked myself what I had learned from this experience. Clearly, at least in the near future, I was not likely to return to politics. As a practical matter, I needed to resume gainful activity, and there were no plausible elections on the horizon to pursue, even if the spirit — or something closer to insanity — still moved me. More to the point, as I thought about it, I had to confess that my political foray had earned me more than one kick to the stomach without bringing that other "fire in the belly" that propels the truest of candidates to go back for more. I thought more about what really drove me, and where I seemed to fit best.

I never answered that question with any sort of real conclusion or plan. Yet soon, I began to gravitate toward a new volunteer activity that was just beginning to bring together local community leaders around an effort to establish our region's credentials as an emerging biotechnology center. I had learned of this initiative during my campaign, and also gotten to know many of the business and university leaders interested in advancing it. Though I returned to my law firm and the duty of putting in (and billing) my hours, I began to put even more of my energy into this new outside activity, ultimately getting my firm's blessing to serve as a volunteer to put a new organization and funding in place. At some point, it dawned on me that the despair had passed, that I was more or less back on track and could at least now get up every day and begin to see myself as someone involved in something that (in my own terms, which are always the ones that matter most) might make a difference. Not surprisingly, this new activity had many elements of the old: I found myself back constructing a campaign of sorts — but this time, not for political office but for new investments and new jobs. Within four years, I had left my law firm behind and signed on as the president of a new organization that offered a focus on building biotechnology enterprises and raising the required capital to do so. It was hard work, but it was work I was overall well suited to attempt. Slowly, the pieces began to make sense in a whole new pattern for me.

In recounting this journey, I wish to make it sound neither more significant nor more coherent than it has been. The process was long and fitful, and on many days it seemed endless. While I do believe that I eventually managed to pick myself up at a tough point and hit upon a new and personally worthy vocational pursuit, my particular brand of religious faith does not insist that I was somehow divinely led through this effort, or to this particular outcome. I had no special vision. I managed only to keep focus. Still, faith played its part by forcing me to keep a sense of perspective. Even in defeat, I was still able to take myself seriously, to believe that what I did might (and should) actually count for something. And so, when it mattered most, my belief kept me from completely giving up the search for value, even after what I always assumed to be my life's "grand purpose" had received such a heavy blow. I never felt good about the results of my political campaign — indeed, it carries a sad and decidedly embarrassing shape when I recall it to this day. But I was able to stay alert for opportunity. And fortunately for me, opportunity did come.

When I think of that opportunity today, I can identify a third reason — beyond basic need and sense of purpose — that my father's brand of religious belief has remained not only so important but also so plausible for me: it fits with the larger pattern of the way I have come to see the rest of life. When I was corresponding with my father from college, I wrote to him seeking definitive knowledge. I was sure, in a way only someone in late adolescence can be sure about anything, that whether in matters of science, sociology, or faith, it was possible for someone like me to master even the most demanding concepts, so long as I had some expert help (like his, when it came to religion) to get me started. While readily acknowledging that I did not have all the answers, I was certain that all those answers could be identified, assembled, and expressed, and that if such a thing was not possible, the subject at hand was simply not worthy or true. My father, however, urged me to build upon a more modest foundation, and to make peace with the notion of believing in a God I could never fully explain — not because God wasn't real, but because people were generally not up to the task of fully understanding him.

Over time, I have come to see his point. With each passing year, I assemble more evidence that, whatever the question, no human approach to it ever seems to do a credible job of finding all the answers. I am increasingly skeptical of the often facile coherence of insistent ideology, whether in politics, science, or religion. The result for me is a type of patience, in which I grow better accustomed to the realization that the failure of our vision does not necessarily make the effort to believe, or the object of our believing, something less worthy or true. As my father taught, what is flawed is not the substance of the belief but, often, the limited perceptions of the believer.

My current job offers particular confirmation of this approach. Frequently over the last few years, I have seen my father's wisdom in the field of religion apply equally in biological science — a realm supposedly in conflict with religion, in part, because science is assumed to be so systematic and sure. From what I have seen, science is anything but those things, and is instead very much (like the rest of us) a work in progress. Perhaps this is why some of the most humble, thoughtful, and, often, religious people I know are scientists.

At least once a week I am visited by a gifted researcher in biology, chemistry, or engineering who asks for investment in what he or she feels certain is a discovery that will lead to the next big cure for cancer, or heart failure, or tuberculosis, or lung disease. Most of these people are demonstrably brilliant, and their work is usually intellectually compelling to the point of being overwhelming. But I have seen, over the past several years, that as promising as these discoveries may be, most of them will not be successful. Because the discoverers' newfound knowledge won't work the way they think it will. Something will go wrong. Some theory about how a drug affects the human body, or how one of our genes can be altered to make us grow tissue or stop producing cancer cells, will turn out to be just that — an elegant theory, but never a reality.

Here again, as in matters of religious faith, it isn't that our impressions are wrong, or that these scientists aren't truly intelligent, or dedicated, or creative. It's just that none of us yet knows enough, and there is so much left to learn before anyone can really put even the science we think we know, today, to work.

Never was this made clearer to me than when, in late 2006, I was invited to a meeting at the Ann Arbor, Michigan, facilities of Pfizer, one of the nation's largest pharmaceutical companies. Like many other major pharmaceutical companies today, Pfizer is increasingly eager to learn of scientific discoveries that might soon be translated into new products. The midwestern United States, with its many great research universities and federally funded laboratories, is especially fertile ground for such a quest, and Pfizer regularly convened regional conferences of organizations like mine that are involved in finding and funding promising new companies. On this particular occasion, as it turned out, the need for innovation was especially urgent. The preceding week, Pfizer had suffered one of the greatest, and most expensive, failures ever recorded in the development of potential blockbuster products — an investment representing years of effort and well over $800 million, all for naught.

The story is almost as simple as it is sad. For many years, Pfizer had exclusive rights to the cardiovascular drug Lipitor, at that time the most successful medicine ever to be marketed, bringing in billions of dollars in revenue year after year. Lipitor and drugs in a similar class called statins fight heart disease by lowering the so-called bad cholesterol (LDL) that leads to the buildup of fat deposits, called plaque, in the arteries of millions of patients worldwide. With Lipitor's patent set to expire in a few short years, Pfizer determined to build on its franchise by improving it. Several years earlier the company had announced progress on a new drug that, when combined with the properties of Lipitor, would fight heart disease even more effectively by further lowering LDL and also, conveniently, raising the so-called good cholesterol (HDL) that is thought to be one of the body's best natural defenses against plaque deposits. (I recall explaining to my teen-aged daughter at the time that Pfizer was working on a drug that, in true Harry Potteresque fashion, would combine the body's "good wizards" and "bad wizards" to come up with a potent cure.) Early tests of the new drug were highly promising, and Pfizer's president promised this new therapy would rank "among the most important new developments for heart disease in decades."

New drugs are developed through a series of clinical trials involving human subjects that test for both safety and effectiveness. Every hurdle a drug clears in its path to approval is increasingly higher, that is, the complexity of the trial and the number of tested subjects involved steadily increase.

Just before Pfizer was set to make its final application for approval to the U.S. Food and Drug Administration, the results of the last round of clinical trials came in. Press accounts at the time recorded this remarkable story. Over the course of a single dramatic weekend, the status of Pfizer's next major medicine for cardiovascular disease plummeted from the heights of "likely next blockbuster" to the cellar of a failed experiment. The clinical trials had revealed a highly unforeseen but equally unacceptable risk of death among treated subjects, when compared with others not given the drug. Pfizer responded expeditiously and unequivocally, announcing the drug's summary withdrawal and a complete loss of the nearly $1 billion the company had invested in its development.

In the wake of this failure, Pfizer abandoned not only the new drug but also most of its pipeline of potential new cardiovascular products. Later, Pfizer sold its cardiovascular research laboratories, shut down most of its research programs in heart disease, and refocused its efforts in other areas. All these events were beginning to unfold at the time of my Michigan conference. During one session, when asked to explain this sudden set of actions, one of Pfizer's bewildered scientists responded with unusual candor: "I really don't know how to answer that. While we thought we understood a great deal about how heart disease affects people, there's a lot we don't know after all. The drug should have worked. It didn't. There just isn't any good explanation."

In this case, it is probably true that in the end, nothing was actually wrong with the drug. Nor was probably anything wrong with the study design or procedures involved in the clinical trials that led to such unfortunate results. And most likely, there was nothing new (or at least unforeseen) that was wrong with the patients who were part of those trials, even the ones that died during the process. The problem was with the science — the theory of heart disease, the theory that Pfizer thought was clear and obvious enough to justify spending nearly a billion dollars to pursue, the theory that was for some mysterious reason . . . simply . . . wrong.

More accurately, the theory was wrong because it was based on incomplete knowledge. For me, what this signifies is both familiar and, somehow, almost comforting: the same challenge of "seeing through a glass darkly" that clouds our vision of God also confounds our knowledge of his creation. It is not that our beliefs — or our knowledge — are untrue. It is literally that we are not capable, at least as we now are, of comprehending the entire truth, and we are frankly foolish to expect things to be otherwise. We have no choice but to go on experimenting, learning, building on what we do know, and advancing in our understanding, just as we have no choice but to go on believing in a God who is a critical but not always comprehensible part of our lives. It seems that as human beings, we can never gain the comfort of certainty that we have truly figured anything out. There's always something we're missing. There's always something that doesn't quite add up. So we need to focus on the parts that work, and try to make them work better for us, whether in science or in religious belief.

I can, of course, still recall the appealing ring of my adolescent drive for certainty. Particularly when it comes to reli-

gion, I readily acknowledge my ongoing wish for keener powers of perception. As my father observed, we see parts of our
belief in our lives, and in the lives of others, that we know to
be real and valid. Yet often we cannot understand how these
parts are all put together. It's frustrating. Over time, I've
come to appreciate how much that frustration can shape
someone's approach to faith. Sometimes, in fact, we respond
by going overboard, giving in to the temptation to see patterns that just aren't there, to insist upon a level of certainty
that simply can't be, to pound the pieces together into something we insist is the whole truth because we know there
must be a whole truth. I understand this passion and the
good intentions behind it, but I work even harder to avoid
giving in to it. Because in doing so, we risk an approach to
faith that is more of an ideological construct than a road map
that can really help us find and navigate the rugged terrain of
our lives. As ideology drives us further afield, we can lose
touch with basic reasoning and the reassuring fellowship of
others. My father captured such a moment — and its frustration — in another of his letters.

> I'm finding that sometimes when people come up against
> a wall in their faith, they respond by claiming beliefs they
> refuse to discuss rationally at all. Religion to them then
> departs wholly from reason, and becomes a matter of
> sheer emotion. You may remember one of my favorite
> church elders, Mr. J———, who after a period of great
> distress in his life and much counseling by me, suddenly
> wrote me a letter resigning from the session [ruling body
> of elders] and from the church. He told me in his letter

that in response to his quest for God, he had now received the gift of speaking in tongues, and now knows that God is very close to him. He added, in his letter to me, "The verse of scripture which I take as my authority is 1 Corinthians 14:2 — 'For one who speaks in a tongue speaks not to men but to God. . . .'" I talked to him after I received his letter and I asked him, "Why did you stop at the semicolon in that verse? Why didn't you read on? In verses two and three, this is what I read: 'For one who speaks in a tongue speaks not to men but to God; for no one understands him, but he utters mysteries in the Spirit. On the other hand, he who prophesies (preaches) speaks to men for their upbuilding and encouragement and consolation.'" Do you know what he said to me? He said, "I stopped there because that is as far as the Holy Spirit led me." Now how do you argue against that kind of logic and biblical interpretation? You can't!

Through his very last days, my father never felt he had to suspend his considerable intellectual powers when it came to questions of belief. Indeed, he never found any essential conflict between logic and faith, or between science and religion. In part, he could avoid such conflict because he could discern, in each approach to knowledge, a credible and complementary approach to truth. But he could also harmonize the scientific and religious perspectives because in each case he knew that the ultimate receiving instrument — the human mind — had such limited powers to comprehend at anything like a level of reliable certainty. Thus, truth must be understood imperfectly, and in multiple dimensions.

His was an approach to belief that fell, deliberately, several paces short of a system. He found it important most of all for religion to "stay real" through insights and experiences that can be warmly given, reliably tested, and credibly explained. I share this way of looking at belief. It continues to make sense to me today. I have also found, however, that for my own belief to have lasting substance, something even more is required: active expression through a relationship called faith.

The Second Lesson

LEAPING TO FAITH

Like many my age, I have become a reluctant expert in the American health-care system. My knowledge has come about not from direct experience (yet) with any health challenges of my own, but through caring for two aging — and eventually, dying — parents. I have now seen both hospitals and hospices up close, and learned to understand the differences between them in levels of expectation, intervention, and care.

Both my parents lived relatively long and healthy lives. Each of them died a difficult death. In my father's case, because his cancer was discovered so late, the outcome was certain long before the discovery was made. Beyond any real chance of survival, my father's clear course of treatment (which, fortunately, he was a full participant in choosing) was hospice care, watching and waiting for the end, trying to stay as comfortable and unharried as possible. As a family member, I liked much about hospice care, including the extended periods when my father was simply left in peace by the medical staff and his family had ready access to long, uninterrupted time with him. It was sad and difficult. At the end, he was clearly in pain. Mercifully, he slept. But I knew what to do at the hospice. Showing up and standing by were the principal activities required of me.

My mother's challenges were longer-lasting, and more complex. Suffering for many years from a bad heart and slowly progressing congestive heart failure, she eventually ended up in intensive care, battling minute by minute to find enough oxygen to draw her next breath. She was fully conscious, right up until the very end, and fiercely resistant to either decline or death. Her treatment required much of her family, involving a series of moves to various levels of care in the hospital; constant coordination of multiple (and seemingly disconnected) medical specialists, where no one really seemed to be in charge; and agonizing decisions by me, as the son on the scene with power of attorney, as to how much intervention was warranted, and how much the inevitable end should be postponed. I never knew what to do at the hospital. Every day when I visited my mother, it seemed there was some new, painful choice to make.

But of the two experiences, I preferred the hospital. I preferred it because there was always something very hard to do but also something still at stake. Something that kept everything and everyone disrupted because there remained just a chance that my mother's condition could improve and the end be forestalled. I preferred the hospital because it was still about life, in all of its messiness and chaos. The hospital permitted hope.

In my experience, Christians often come in either the "hospital" or "hospice" visitor variety. Some have a desire mainly to find a belief, to settle into it, and then to hold on to it. The fact that, once inside this shelter, nothing should be at stake beyond — and because of — the "certainty" of salvation is the greatest source of comfort. Doctrine and ideology are important, and add a type of intellectual rigor to the structure. Faith is overwhelmingly therapeutic, a continuous healing process whose principal demand is showing up for care and standing firm. These are hospice Christians, and their approach to faith, though deliberately self-limiting, can also be enviably self-fulfilling.

For others, Christianity comes in a far messier form. Though they frequently question whether they live up to the title, these are indeed "Christians" holding strong elements of belief. But such belief is usually commingled with doubt, and often exhibits a demonstrable lack of intellectual consistency or systematic thinking. It can be extremely difficult for these Christians to say what exactly it is — and what it isn't — that they believe. Faith involves not clarity but activity, giving rise to a constant barrage of assorted efforts, including Bible studies, small group sessions, and Sunday morning services. These are restless practitioners, constantly working on what they believe — and constantly worried they are not more "religious." These are hospital Christians.

As much as I envy the certainty of hospice Christians, I am definitely a Christian of the hospital variety. I come by this honestly. My father also approached his faith as a necessarily tumultuous affair, pointing out that tumult was inevitable because relationships are always difficult to understand, define, and manage, and faith involves nothing less than a direct, ongoing relationship with a truly personal authority — Jesus Christ:

> We need in Christianity personal commitment, not only to what Christ, our authority, teaches, but to Christ the authority himself. Because what we are talking about here is something far larger than belief. It's what Christians call *faith*. Many people think that faith means believing something you know is not true, or at least very improbable. But faith really means *being faithful*, conscientiously committed, steadfastly trying to pattern your life after what you have accepted from and seen in the teacher. And that's why Dietrich Bonhoeffer could say that faith is obedience, and obedience is faith.

This "working" approach to Christianity was credible to me when my father first offered it over thirty-five years ago. For me now, it remains credible because it most accurately reflects how I take those actions and make those decisions in my own life, where all the cards are on the table. I see faith as a relationship rather than simply a belief. I experience faith as a set of expectations, hopes, challenges, ambitions, disappointments, and surprises encountered along the way, rather than as an immutable, defining principle. Such an approach makes sense to me because it reflects how I act in every other aspect of my life where decisions have consequences and today's actions truly matter.

Drawing on another part of my experience, I realize that I arrive at not only my religious convictions but also my professional investment decisions on a basis that looks a lot more like faith than belief. As I noted earlier, the start-up investment fund I oversee typically makes the very first significant financial commitment to what has been, up to this point, an intriguing but totally unproven proposal for a new company in biotechnology or health care. All start-up companies involve enormous amounts of risk; human enterprises never unfold the way we envision them, with everything taking more time and more money than anyone could possibly have predicted. Add to this shaky foundation the fact that the science upon which biotechnology start-ups are based is almost always novel and largely untested, and the further fact that all new products destined for ingestion or incorporation into the human body must be thoroughly and repeatedly tested by federal regulatory authorities — and it's small wonder that only one in one hundred of these "great discoveries" ever attracts funding, or that fewer than one in ten of those that get funded ever enjoy any measure of validation or success.

Still, every so often a company comes along with a great idea that can literally change, extend, or at least improve the quality of life as we know it. Thanks to the advances made by start-up biotechnology companies over the last twenty-five years, many forms of cancer are now fully treatable, AIDS has gone from a death sentence to a chronic disease, and heart attacks can often be avoided with simple implanted devices instead of dangerous and disruptive surgery. The risk is always high, but once in a while the reward is astronomically higher.

Our fund has now made twelve investments (out of nearly two hundred "opportunities") in these types of high-potential, high-risk companies, each aiming against the odds to succeed in filling some compelling, unmet medical need. To date, each of our companies is surviving, and many have attracted additional funds from others. But all face years of uncertainty ahead — literally seeking to steer a course through what investors reliably and without irony term the "valley of death" — before patients (or investors) will see a successful result. And of course, the odds are high that many, if not most, of these companies will never succeed at all.

So how do we choose where to invest — where to place our bets?

Recently we were visited by a four-person team of scientists and entrepreneurs who proposed that we step forward as the very first investor in their new company, on the basis of years of diligent scientific research into a novel pathway for deploying drugs to find and kill cancer cells while leaving healthy cells alone. Many similar efforts are now under way to find such a holy grail for cancer cures, all based on the theory that the anticancer toxins we have already discovered often work pretty well at killing tumors but, unfortunately, work equally well at killing healthy tissue, organs, and any other system in the body that depends upon the rapid repair or rapid growth of cells (think about friends or family on chemotherapy who lose all their hair, simply because hair cells multiply quickly to keep hair growing). Thus, if someone can come up with a way, some back door, to target cancer cells — and only cancer cells — for a fatal cocktail of anticancer drugs that leaves healthy tissue alone, then the cocktail can be made very strong, with the chances of terminating the tumor far higher. It's an elegant theory; there are glimmers of evidence that it might really work, and many brilliant scientists seeking to make it so.

When we heard about this company, the chairman of our investment committee (a distinguished scientific researcher in his own right, among many other professional accomplishments) asked probing questions. Finally, he declared the science to be "novel and interesting." But as even he pointed out, the research was very early, the findings were very preliminary, and nothing had ever been tested on an actual human subject. We were, in short, captivated by science we all found compelling; we wanted to "believe"; but that desire alone was not enough to make us invest.

Yet we did invest. In the end, we based our decision not on the science, but on our ability to form an opinion about, and ultimately to form a relationship with, the entrepreneurial team prepared to build a company around that science. This was a credible, experienced, approachable group, with nicely complementary scientific, business, and financial experience and skills. They were all trying to build something completely new, of course, yet they brought to the effort familiar and comforting human attributes of resourcefulness, energy, integrity, and seasoned optimism. Two of them had even succeeded in building similarly novel companies before. On our part, we could neither directly nor competently comprehend, let alone believe, the science, no matter how much we wanted to do so. But what we could do is come to know, and have faith in, the company team — and through their efforts, and our ongoing relationship with them, come to understand the science a little better, hopefully to see it in action and to witness its work. We could therefore "relate" to the vision by relating to the people — a very common practice in making these types of investment decisions. As one commentator on biotechnology investing once put it, "You have a choice to bet on the horse, or to bet on the jockey; I usually place my money on the jockey."

To me, this is also how, as Christians, we place our "bet" on our belief in God — by seeing in Christ someone and something we can understand, someone with whom we can envision a relationship and, by building upon that relationship, come to know much more about the object and purpose of our belief. My father cast an image to make this point beautifully in one of his letters: "As you know, I was born and raised on Little Bay de Noc in Michigan's Upper Peninsula. Little Bay de Noc was like Lake Michigan; their waters were the same. What I saw and felt in the waters of the bay was true of the lake. But there was more to Lake Michigan than the limited view I had of it from Little Bay de Noc."

One thing that troubled me early on about this "relationship to God through Christ" basis of Christianity was understanding the initial relationship between two of the essential participants — God and Christ. Many, I believe, stumble with the overall credibility of the Christian message because they find the whole notion of the Trinity, or "God in three persons," to be a circuitous riddle that does not leave a clear picture of what God is truly like — or for that matter, which "version" of God we're supposed to believe in, and relate to. When my father and I corresponded, I pressed him hard on this point, urging him to give me clear direction on whether Christ was "more human" or "more divine." I wanted some indication of an objective ordering of things that was concrete and true, so I would know where Christ fit — and then where God fit — and of course where I fit in the whole equation. As I look back on it now, he wisely demurred, offering a far more nuanced explanation of the nature of Christ, and Christ's relationship to God.

You see, I believe that the concept of the human-divine nature of Christ and the concept of the Trinity are the results of human endeavor to give form or substance to ideas we can't express any other way. We experience God as the Creator; we experience God in Christ; we experience God as a spirit present in our lives. So, we try to put our experience of God into a formula, a concept, a phrase, and we come up with the idea of the Trinity. I'm not sure God in his real being is a Trinity. That concept is simply our attempt to describe what we experience. The same can be said, I think, of the nature of Christ, both human and divine. I experience him as a man; I experience him as a God. So, I come up with my statement of belief, my creed. But I'm not sure the creed describes Christ as what he really is. How do I describe myself — son, father, husband, brother, man? I'm all these things; but I'm so much more than just the content of those words.

My father went on to suggest that, at certain times, we may favor one partial vision of the truth over another, because we need the guidance that this vision provides; but the truth remains complex and ineffable, just as every important thing — in this world or beyond — must be.

In the relationship I have with Jesus, he meets my personal needs as they arise. There are days when I need to know he is a complete, flesh and blood man, subject to all the same temptations, the same hopes, the same fears that I am. In those days, I see him as a man. There are other times when I feel the need of being forgiven, when I feel the need of having someone in charge, someone with power and authority to speak to me of this life and of the life to come. In those times, I suppose, I turn to my feeling of his divinity. I'm not sure it is of ultimate importance to say that Christ is either God or man; or that he is completely God and completely man. It seems so limiting to have to put this into words. Can't we just say, as we look at Christ: "Man can be like that"? Can't we just say, as we look at Christ: "God is like that"?

At the time my father wrote those words to me, I saw them as almost an intellectual dodge, a refusal to make a stand on an important intellectual point. Now, they seem profound, whole and three-dimensional, because they describe not only faith as I can credibly experience it, but also life as I actually live it — and make the appropriate connection between the two.

In fact, as I now reflect on the visions of Jesus in the New Testament that give me comfort and confirmation, I realize that what I find credible or comforting about Christ has shifted with age. When I was younger and charged with youthful ambition — including late adolescence, when I was corresponding with my father — I found Christ's statements of power and authority to be inspiring above all. I loved the fact that, in the Gospel accounts, this was no self-effacing Superman, coming to earth but constantly seeking to temper his divine powers and shield his true identity behind the meek and mild demeanor of some carpentry version of Clark Kent. No, he proclaimed and he demonstrated his power and glory. I cheered the Jesus of the miracles, the multiplier of loaves and fishes, the triumphant victor over Satan in the desert, the Jesus who threw the money changers out of the temple and left zero ambiguity regarding his divine and therefore eternal status when he declared, "Very truly, I tell you, before Abraham was, I am" (John 8:58).

This vision of a God who can take charge, and be truly "godlike" when it counts, is still energizing for me. But my youthful enthusiasm missed my father's far more profound point, about a God so powerful he could choose to join his creation fully, literally, in time and in love:

> Think about a Christ that was born and came into the world as we do. He was flesh and blood and bone as we are. The physical weariness he felt was real. His tears were actual, salty human tears. He could grow angry as we do, and needed love and friendship like any human being. His temptations were as many and as real as ours, and when he suffered body and soul on the cross, it was real, poignant suffering. On every page of the Gospels, there emerges someone whose humanity is unmistakable. Such a Christ not only speaks for God, but says a lot about him.

Indeed he does. Today, I find special affirmation in those moments of the Gospel accounts when Christ just unmistakably goes on record as someone who identifies with the routine frustrations of the humanity he has come to join. Within the parables, the wisdom, and the tough love of Christ's words to followers and foes, there are also confirming — and highly quotable — insights into the everyday human experience. I take real comfort in Christ's ironic quip, "Truly I tell you, no prophet is accepted in the prophet's hometown" (Luke 4:24) (how often in business do we conclude that we need some expensive national expert to give us a report on things we already know?), or his exasperated question, "Why do you call me 'Lord, Lord,' and do not do what I tell you?" (Luke 6:46) (what parent has not felt and said exactly the same to his or her child a hundred times over?). And I know far better today than I could possibly have appreciated nearly forty years ago the worldly wisdom in the words "The spirit indeed is willing, but the flesh is weak" (Matt. 26:41). The Christ who indulges these emotions, speaks these words, observes these human foibles is a Christ who seems terribly "real" to me. He knows very well not only the details of our lives but also the details of our approach to life. Not only can I believe in him — I can relate to him.

And relationships are usually pretty interesting. They're about two parties, and those parties and the circumstances around them change over time. Relationships are fluid, not fixed or rigid, and if they're good, they more often bring the parties together than put distance between them. Given that such a relationship was possible, I struggled in those letters I wrote my father so long ago — and still do — to understand why some Christians insist on making Christ seem so two-dimensional, why they try to "pin him down" and make every word attributed to him into law or doctrine, rather than accounts of real words to real people in a more living document.

My father also puzzled over this fundamentalist approach to Christianity. "Unfortunately," he observed, "most people think that to be true Christians, we have to be odd and dull and pious. Instead of being joyous and winsome, they try to be more religious than Jesus (who was certainly not very religious)."

He was right about that. And from childhood, it has seemed to me that the New Testament offers more hope for openly imperfect seekers than for naively confident purists. Like their secular counterparts two millennia hence, the religious lawyers or Pharisees come off especially poorly in these accounts. In fact, whole chapters of Matthew and Luke are dedicated to their denunciation. Consider: "But woe to you, scribes and Pharisees, hypocrites! For you lock people out of the kingdom of heaven. For you do not go in yourselves, and when others are going in, you stop them" (Matt. 23:13-14). And in the Gospels, even more seemingly approachable "religious civilians," who thought they had figured out what they needed to do, very clearly came up short. Recall the petitioner who asked Jesus what he must do to gain eternal life, and glowed with pride as he recited his fidelity to all the biblical commandments — only to be told that he would not inherit eternal life until he gave up everything he had, all his worldly accomplishments, and followed Christ. Predictably, when he heard this, the petitioner "was shocked and went away grieving, for he had many possessions" (Mark 10:19-22).

The Gospels are filled with these sketches of people, some vain and pious, some simply closed and clueless, who just "don't get it." These accounts contrast with others about those who, though "not getting" all of it, do appreciate the simpler point that when it comes to Jesus, something is indeed happening. And something is at stake; they must ask, listen, and follow; and they must be open to change. They must, in fact, be open to the relationship of faith.

Why then do some Christians continue to focus on finding immutable words, codes, and commandments in the New Testament — when the Gospels emphasize the much harder, but more creative, requirement to express belief, to seek God out, through an active relationship? Why would anyone want to look as rigid as a Pharisee — to appear to be all about laws and literal interpretations — when Christ is demanding a far more iterative, evolving engagement with him? I couldn't answer this question when my father and I were corresponding. Over thirty-five years later, I still can't.

When I consider this question in a more routine context, I think of the many business negotiations I handled on behalf of clients over many years of legal practice. Invariably, in any deal involving significant sums of money, there were numerous lawyers, and they entered the discussion with a wide variety of approaches. Some pounded the table. Some held their cards close. And some decided they could gain special advantage by being the "smartest person in the room," the obvious master of all the laws at stake and all the facts in play. They sought to demonstrate their command of the rules, and thereby assure their command of the field. Certainly, it is true that these "by the book" lawyers sometimes prevail — because they do indeed turn out to have the law on their side, in situations where success hinges on who is literally right.

But in my experience — even though the law is always important, and always demands full compliance — there are relatively few black and white disagreements, where the outcome is ultimately decided by what's legally permitted or possible. More likely, the outcome of a negotiation will be determined by what people decide they can live with, or put up with, or otherwise feel good about getting at the end of the day. And in these types of negotiations, the lawyers who prevail are often those who are clearly skilled in the law but also, most of all, possess some additional element that allows them to connect with the people involved to reach an outcome.

It is not that these lawyers please everyone, or become the friend of all. If they are ethical (and contrary to popular belief, most lawyers I know really try to be so), they always make it clear that they have a client, and therefore a bias in the argument. But they manage to relate to the whole situation. In the end, they usually win because they appear to be reasonable in their approach to an outcome, and succeed in compelling a reasonable response. In these cases, the contract is sealed — the law is made — not by a code citation but through the relationship these lawyers can establish with all pertinent parties to get to a result that seems to make the most sense. In legal practice, I always aspired to be one of this breed of lawyers. And I always feared to come up against one as an adversary.

Over time, I have come to believe with growing conviction that Christianity binds us to the miracle of God's grace, but succeeds in doing so through the familiar pathways of everyday life. We believe in what, and who, we can encounter and engage. We are moved by relationships, by others who connect with us. And we move in faith because we can believe in a God with whom we can have a complex, living, and hopeful relationship as "hospital Christians." Out of the assurance that we are known and loved, we can believe in a God who can teach us how to act — and how to love.

The Third Lesson

LOVE TO THE LIMITS

F rom our earliest days, in Sunday school classes and by simple songs, we are taught that "God is love." We learn from our childhood Bible training that God loved the world so much that he sent his only Son to us, as both a gift and a challenge to love him back — and to love others as well. We are asked, therefore, to believe that the driving energy of the universe is the warmth of a beating heart, loving us from the beginning of time, and for all time, in the way we understand that word "love." As children, we take comfort from this vision; we see God as ultimately kind and gentle, and the vast universe as, somehow, friendly.

As most of us get older, this vision of God becomes harder to square with what we observe around us every day. We see Haitian earthquakes and Indonesian tsunamis, and ask how a loving God could let such massive suffering happen. We see a succession of poor and struggling countries ruled by demonic dictators, bringing all-too-familiar cycles of corruption, executions, hunger, 10,000 percent inflation, and no functioning economy. We witness the carnage caused by terrorists. And we begin to wonder why a loving God just didn't "make us better," so that people would not treat each other so hatefully. We see shallow views prevail, cynics too often rewarded for low expectations of others, and kind actions consistently rebuffed.

Proceeding down this path, many of us begin to suspect that in the end — and, perhaps, from the beginning — the essential character of the world is not warm and loving after all. The natural state of all things everywhere is cold. We are alone. We can go through life huddled in the dark around the fire with a few fellow travelers. But in the end, we're on our own in a universe that neither knows nor cares about us. The image of a glowing Jesus surrounded by adoring little children, idealized from Gospel accounts, becomes more and more a picture to be left on the walls of an infant's nursery, and ceases to be a vision of anything that can be relied upon in the adult world. It is not only belief in a God of love that seems to fly in the face of reality, but belief in God at all. For many, arriving at atheism or agnosticism happens not through some process of reasoned discourse or rational debate. Often, we cease to believe just from sheer disappointment.

My father had a lifelong, vigorous engagement with the concept of a truly loving God. He did believe in a God of love. Yet as a pastor, he freely acknowledged that this belief provided him with at least as many questions as answers: "This issue of how so much evil can exist in a loving world may not be crucial to some academic theologians, but I tell you this: it is crucial to pastors like me. When you deal with a suffering human being trying to maintain his faith in a just and good God in the face of some unexplainable and over-powering tragedy, then you see what spiritual agony and religious despair are all about."

As I will discuss in more detail later, my father never came close to answering those basic questions, at least for himself. Still, he did arrive at some basic conclusions about the loving relationship of faith between God and his creation that he passed on to me in his letters, and then continued to work on throughout the rest of his ministry.

He began with the conviction that the Bible, Old and New Testaments taken together, presents the story of God not only as prime mover but very much as historical actor. More-over, he found this to be a God who not only intervenes in time but also has fundamentally changed his relationship with his creation over time to make an ultimate declaration of love: "I believe that God created human beings for fellow-ship with him. Genesis suggests as much. But that purpose of God's was thwarted when his children, with their inherent freedom, went their own way and disobeyed."

He consequently viewed the Old Testament as essentially the story of a frustrated father "trying to reclaim his errant and straying children." For God, that Old Testament effort took a series of escalating steps: "At first, God tried to get rid of the trouble-makers — hence the story of Noah and the ark, where only a remnant was preserved. But even the blessed remnant went astray and we are led to the (I suspect) mythic tale of the Tower of Babel, where God scattered mankind into many languages and nations. Then we see him bargaining, and the making of promises between Father and child."

Then the lawyers got involved. "God made an agreement — a covenant — with Abraham. It contained rules and promises. But unfortunately, the covenant failed, and human beings reverted to rebellion, anarchy, idolatry, and sin. More laws were made and commandments given. But these also eventually failed."

God's intervention grew more direct. "Counselors — prophets — were called in to lead God's children to the right. But here again was disappointment and defeat."

The result was an Old Testament record of "a disappointed parent, baffled and frustrated at every turn."

The New Testament is, in my father's view, the record of God's decision to engage his creation very differently. This time, God didn't seek to command or contract with people, or even attempt to persuade them indirectly from afar; he decided to join people, right here.

The God of the New Testament says, "Now, I am taking the final step. I come to you in my beloved Son, Jesus. I come to love you into faithfulness and obedience. You did not know how much I loved and cared, how far I was willing to go to bring you home. Now you know. I am willing for my only son, heart of my very heart, to suffer and die for you. In very reality, I suffer and die through him. What more can I say to you? What more can I do for you? I am a God who weeps! Yes, of course I have the power to cancel out the whole thing. Yes, I could start again. But I still think there's a chance here with you. I still think there is hope here with you. And so I persist, loving to the very end."

Many years later, I find my father's likening the Bible story to the saga of a dysfunctional family to be instructive, and sadly appropriate for today. It suggests that over millennia, God has had as much trouble understanding and communicating with us as we have with him. And it provides a context that makes the advent of Christ seem even more profound, as God places everything, including his very authority, on the line for the love of his creation. We may never be able to understand all the aspects of God's love. But in Reverend Johnson's view, we cannot doubt what the Bible is trying to say about that love's totality through this ultimate expression in Christ. Believing in a God who could send Christ becomes easier for me to fathom when I, as a father myself, contemplate the lengths to which distraught parents will go — beyond all reason, and past anyone's understanding (perhaps, including our own) — to rescue their children from threat, danger, or loss.

My father's second conclusion was that God's revealed love for us, and our love for him, are designed to be cast as muscular verbs rather than fuzzy nouns. He noted in one of his letters that "When the apostle Paul speaks of the love of God, he never does so by speaking of love as an emotion. Instead, the Greek word that Paul uses in his letters to Corinth and other early churches is the word *agape*. It is the word that Christ also used in speaking of love."

My father believed the use of this particular term was no accident or error in translation. "The Greeks had other words for love, words like *eros* and *philos* that have emotional content. But *agape* is different; it thinks of love as an acting out, rather than a feeling. Love is being loving. Love is doing loving things. Paul would say, 'If I tell you I love you, the real test of the truth of my words is not how I feel, but what I do.'" My father went on to observe that, when Christians understand God's love in this way and see the sending of Christ in this light, they are more likely to be open to expressing their love — their faith — through "disciplined action and willing obedience rather than a shallow, wordy, emotional relationship with God that lacks theological depth and social significance."

As an adult convert to Calvinist Christianity, my father placed high value in notions of discipline and obedience. Over the course of my life, I have found the "discipline" of loving to be very important for my own identity as well.

I am convinced that, without this priority and approach, the adult I have become would have veered off the tracks of open, accepting behavior long ago. Like most of us, I am by nature a self-centered, self-seeking person. I genuinely enjoy the company of others, and quickly shrivel without it. Yet I confess I am still not one of those who is naturally garrulous, openly emotional, or, unfortunately, very inspired to demonstrate great wit in most social situations. Without the organizing belief — to a theological certainty — that my faith calls me to be loving, to go out of my way to act for others and to feel genuine concern for their needs and their lives, I would find it far easier to do far less. I would succumb more often to the temptation not to give time, or money, or support to charitable causes under the rationalization that "what one person does can't make much difference in the grand scheme of things." I would be far more inclined to pay less attention to what others are saying in a conversation, because I would be operating on (and drawing considerable comfort from) the assumption that, first and foremost and in the end, my only true interest was in myself.

The love of God that sent Christ is neither passive nor comfortable. It is, above all else, constantly challenging. If I believe it at all, my behavior changes, my view of what's important extends insistently outside myself, even on those (many) days that I don't feel especially warm, loving, or sociable. I may give grudgingly; I may really wish to be left alone. Yet as a Christian, seeing what God has done through Christ, I'm just a whole lot less at ease telling myself that it's all right to be selfish. Christianity stubbornly keeps not only God, but also other people, right in the middle of the picture.

In finding the right picture for our focus, we also need to check to be sure we are fully in it. After all, we are called to respond to our Christian faith by doing more than simply developing better manners, mastering the art of more socially acceptable, "extroverted behavior" toward others. Indeed, if we are truly seeking to give of ourselves, then we should be engaging others with the best of ourselves. We should give this relationship all we can, by deploying the specific gifts that God has bestowed on us — those talents, insights, and attitudes — that present us uniquely as who we are in our best lights.

Recently I heard a sermon on that ever-troubling text for relatively affluent Christians, "For where your treasure is, there your heart will be also" (Matt. 6:21). With considerable passion, the pastor employed this passage to discuss how Christians can often embark upon "false missions." He noted that many of us believe that by drawing upon what we perceive to be our basic talents, such as articulateness, humor, technical proficiencies, or analytical strengths, we convince ourselves we are glorifying God when, in truth, we are often simply displaying ourselves. The pastor countered that the point of faith is not to be blinded by our own self-absorption, but to give ourselves over completely to the power and wonder of God. Our mission as Christians, therefore, must come from God, and from the teachings of Christ — not from our own drive to impress others or, somehow, to try to impress God.

I suppose the sermon was fine, as far as it went; the point was to place God and others first, putting our egos and ambitions to the side in the process. Still, something large was missing in this message — namely, the complete "us" that is supposed to be giving, and given over, to God and through God to others in our relationship of faith.

By way of example, I think of one of my wife's most remarkable gifts. Here is someone compellingly smart, funny, deeply analytical, and highly compassionate toward others. She has excelled in her education, her professional training, and her profession, and is truly one of those "twenty-first-century women" whose very success is daily putting an end to traditional assumptions that the world will forever be run by men. She puts all these talents to good use as she runs a critical and complex component of a very large company, and is regularly called upon to provide strong and thoughtful leadership at a turbulent time. She's also a great cook — and baker. Trained as she grew up at home, and later through occasional classes and courses, she can make magic out of the most basic ingredients. She doesn't cook for a living, of course — but she surely could. She is also a Christian; and so, does her gift of cooking have any part to play in her Christian service, or is it simply a pleasant distraction from the larger mission?

To argue that hers is a gift fundamentally employed in Christian service is, of course, literally self-serving for me, since I am the beneficiary of so many fine meals. Yet I think of the ways she has put her skills to use in service to others: teaching our five-year-old daughter the meaning of steward-ship by helping her make banana bread for charity bake sales to press upon friends, family, and neighbors week after week in our driveway at home; baking hundreds of chocolate chip cookies for prison inmates as part of a mission project; letting my father know how much she loved him by inviting him and my mother to join us for expert and thoroughly delicious home-cooked meals at least twice a week (my mother had many virtues, but cooking was certainly not among them); showing her staff at work how much she respected (and sim-ply liked) them by inviting them over for home-cooked cui-sine, or taking gourmet pastries into work.

My wife relates to people well, in many successful ways. Certainly, she takes pride in her cooking, as she should. But there is more than pride at work here: cooking has also be-come one of her avenues for communication, for affirmation of affection and respect. In her able hands, cooking becomes a vehicle for service. Along with her many other, and argu-ably more conventional, skills in leadership, generosity, and service, her cooking is indeed a talent put to work in the rela-tionship of faith — as all God-given talents must surely be.

My wife's skill in the kitchen exemplifies another teaching of my father's in the field of Christian love: that the larger promise of faith is often realized through seemingly minor actions and small things. God has taken one ultimate step in sending Christ. In this dance, we respond through a lifetime of discrete, seemingly small actions that let people know we are there for them, or that we care for them, or that, at least, we are listening to them.

For my father, the relationship that best summed up the Christian assignment was marriage: "In marriage, we see every day that love is more than just an emotion. It is honoring another person as a person, respecting another person as a human being, and seeing the other person not just as a functionary (wife, husband, father, mother), but as a real flesh and blood individual with individual needs and aspirations and hopes and sins."

He pointed out the small but significant expressions of love through thoughtful action: "Someone has to work on the budget and someone has to pay the bills; someone must gather the rubbish and someone must clean the house and someone must cut the grass. These may be little, routine, ordinary services that we too often take for granted, but someone has to do them and in doing them, we are expressing our love and dedication for someone else as well."

And most of all, there are the important, small, but constant affirmations of engagement:

We have to work for that faith and tenderness that are mentioned in the marriage ceremony. Romance, tenderness, affection — these things do not come automatically. I think we have to plan for these things and work on them. We need to remember birthdays and holidays and special occasions. Married people need to tell each other every day that they love each other, even on those days when the emotions don't run high. These are the days when our Christian discipline carries us through. To say "I love you" when you don't feel especially loving, helps you to realize that you do indeed love that other person, and you need to start acting that way. It is this really working at being happily married that keeps a marriage warm and tender and filled with affection for "as long as we both shall live."

After my mother's death, I saw many touching reminders of the lengths to which my father went in his own marriage to practice what he preached. He and my mother celebrated their sixtieth wedding anniversary just a few months before his death, and my brother and I threw a party for my parents and their friends that we will always be grateful that we had the foresight — or really, just the good sense — to have for them. Their marriage was a strong one, even though my parents were two very different people. My father was far more outgoing, attention-grabbing, and just plain optimistic about life. My mother brought an opposite approach; she was raised by a stern father (another Presbyterian pastor) to be deferential and "mindful of your place," and was consequently anxious and socially insecure, highly observant, shrewdly analytical, quietly passionate, and remarkably tender. They worked at their marriage, and worked hard to avoid disagreements or fights (my brother and I can never recall hearing them argue, though I suspect that either my memory is selective or my parents were just extremely good at knowing that everything has its particular time and place). True to form, my mother was far less outwardly expressive. Also true to form, my father went out of his way to affirm my mother's place in his life and in our family, and to let her know — often in front of their children — how much she mattered to him.

I used to think that, in a sense, these public expressions of affection were just another part of my father's "show." He was, after all, a public person, a pastor accustomed to saying the right words in front of others to bring out the best in people. But then, buried in some of my mother's preserve of old letters and other mementos, I found a small heap of personal offerings like these:

- A sales slip for a new dress from my father after my mother, evidently, had achieved considerable success on a diet, along with this note (in questionable verse): "My last year's valentine to me / Was wonderful at one-four-three; / while this year's valentine, you know, / Is dearer still at one-two-o! / How to figure if you keep score, / That though you're less I love you more!"
- A somewhat more serious effort, left on my mother's night table, several weeks before their thirty-third wedding anniversary: "Your touch is so tender, / So gently you enmesh my life, / That none but I can ever know / How firmly you clasp / My heart and my happiness / Within the softness of your hand."
- A folded note left in one of my mother's (many) shoes: "I love you from head to foot."
- A note on Mother's Day, nearly forty years into their mar-

riage: "I like special days for you. They give me opportunity to say 'I love you' in a practical way. And I also get to ask you to LUNCH."

- A collage of cut-out paper hearts, arrows piercing each, mounted somewhat crudely on construction paper, with the simple declaration "LOVE YOU," after nearly fifty years of marriage.
- Several dozen other cards, notes, and, inevitably, poems written on numerous anniversaries, Valentine's Days, birthdays, or just random days.

These artifacts were touching, and a bit surprising to me. My father was never gloomy, but he never came across as frothy or frivolous, and most of his poetry (which he wrote a lot) was as earnest as it was highly structured. These verses were more akin to loving doggerel, surely written at the sacrifice of carefully developed standards. I also can't imagine that my mother, cautious and reserved to her core, could ever have reciprocated with notes like these of her own, as much as she was clearly touched to receive and carefully preserve and date every such expression from him.

Knowing this and looking at this pile of affirmations, I was amazed at how hard my father worked, every year and so many times each year, to memorialize his affection for my mother in such a range of thoughtful and even silly ways. He obviously enjoyed the effort. But the important thing was that he just kept at it over more than sixty years of marriage. The results reflected his genuine love for her; they also reflected his fundamental Christian belief in the many ways such love needed constant expression to survive and grow.

Recently, I have had an opportunity to see this truth demonstrated by its counterpoint: what can happen in fundamental relationships when the people involved do not work hard enough at the small but constant affirmations that love requires. Our daughter is a senior at a local Jesuit high school that places strong emphasis upon a highly structured program of student-led spiritual retreats as part of an overall, values-based curriculum. For three days, students are divided into small groups, gain the constant support and overt acceptance of their peers, and typically are wonderfully surprised to receive many long letters of affirming love from parents and other important people in their lives. The students then return to the school on the final evening of the retreat, where they are usually surprised to find parents and family who have been invited to join them for a "debriefing" of what they have experienced.

Our daughter has played an active role in two of these events — one as a retreat participant, the other as a retreat leader. She has found them extremely moving. So have I, especially those debriefing sessions on the final night, when sons and daughters stand up and affirm loved ones who have affirmed them, acknowledge relationships that have gone wrong, and embrace their parents in affection. The words are simple: "Mom, you're the best" or "Dad, even though I never say it, I really love you." Yet in many cases (according to my daughter, who knows much more of the background of these family dramas we briefly witness), these words are being said for the first time after many weeks — or years. The moment is highly emotional, of course, and undoubtedly fleeting, especially for many in the awkward years of adolescence. Yet these words and steps, small and simple, can have lasting impact. They help sustain affection and affirmation if they are just simply communicated, convincingly even if clumsily, from time to time.

On a far less dramatic scale, I think about someone I know in one of the companies I work with on a regular basis. She is someone who makes a real effort to have a good word, or offer a cheerful and often self-effacing line to help others start the day. She is sensitive to colleagues who don't usually get asked about their weekends, or asked to go to lunch. She always seems to me to be going several steps beyond the norm to help others feel a sense of belonging in the office. I don't know her well enough to assert all the reasons she works so hard to be the office optimist, to serve as the friend and confidante to so many. Certainly, it's a conscious decision on her part to act this way. Her own life has real, active sorrow in it, and I am very sure there are many days when she really has to work at it to make herself so engaging. But she succeeds in a way that never feels dramatic or forced — or self-righteous. She told me once that by making an extra effort with people, she enjoys her job far more, and feels better about herself, so that if she is feeling discouraged or depressed, she would rather be at the office than in seclusion. I don't know the specifics of her religious faith, but I know that hers is the essential conduct of a Christian, and that both she and others, if not made whole, are at least somehow made more because of it.

So I continue to share my father's conviction that the Christian relationship of faith is tied to love on the grandest of all possible levels — and on the smallest.

Still, the whole concept that we demonstrate best our love for, or faith with, God through the loving ways we treat others has always seemed to contain a significant "loose end." Certainly, I understand the New Testament concept expressed in such words as Jesus' declaration to his disciples, in Matthew 25:40, "And the king will answer them, 'Truly I tell you, just as you did it to one of the least of these who are members of my family, you did it to me.'" I accept that God's way is the path of love, and that we show our love for God by openly giving it to his creation. But this route to knowing God and affirming a relationship with him has always seemed a bit indirect, reminiscent of what I heard from my parents as a child: "Please get along with your brother. There is nothing that will make us happier than if the two of you get along." I understood, and often responded, to the truth of this statement. Yet, there were times for me then, and there remain moments for me now, that I just want to know much more directly (and yes, selfishly) the state of my own relationship with my "ultimate authority." I may understand that the best way to show my love of God is to love my brother, or other people in my everyday life. I'm ready to acknowledge that these are worthy pursuits, and that God's world is a better place when we treat people as they should be treated. But really, where and how is my primary relationship going with him? Does God know *me* and still love *me?* Am I getting through to him, not just by living right, but somehow by communicating right? Relationships, if they are real, make us dependent and almost needy. We need to be able to check in directly, and make sure that our wife, or our parent — or God — is actually still there and actively still loving us.

Frankly, this level of confirmation has always been hard to come by for me. I suppose this is what going to church, taking time out for stillness and reflection, seeking to communicate and respond through prayer are all meant to do for the aspiring Christian.

Occasionally, it has all come together. Once in a long while, I have been able to be truly quiet and open to true insight. These occasions for me have been regrettably few. Certainly, all are memorable.

Perhaps my clearest moment of feeling God's direct presence, or at least its possibility, came during my time as a graduate student at Oxford University when I went to visit the charming little parish church of Little Gidding, in northern England. An American friend and I, both avid readers in college classes of the poet T. S. Eliot, came to Oxford intrigued by the various English locales that Eliot sought to capture in his major works. During one of our first recess breaks, we decided to take a midwinter pilgrimage by train to Cambridgeshire, where we embarked outside the village of Steeple Gidding and proceeded to the church at the next town, after which one of Eliot's greatest poems is named *(Little Gidding,* the fourth of the *Four Quartets).* Finding Little Gidding was not easy. The search involved walking through the town; proceeding over an active farmyard, across a field and around a barn; skirting a trough; and suddenly, encountering this little jewel box of a church, about sixty feet long and seventeen feet wide.

Built at its present site in the 1600s, the church at Little Gidding has ever since welcomed worshipers and pilgrims, everyone from humble farmers to English royalty (Charles I sought refuge at Little Gidding in 1646 when he was — unsuccessfully, as it turned out — fleeing for his life during the English Civil War). The fact that such an unremarkable place, literally common ground for pigs, Christians, and kings alike, could have been singled out, and thereby redeemed, as an occasional centerpiece for some of history's most intense moments was what captivated T. S. Eliot in *Little Gidding* (". . . for history is a pattern / Of timeless moments. So, while the light fails / On a winter's afternoon, in a secluded chapel / History is now and England"). And anyone who opens the humble door to this poetic setting immediately comes face-to-face with these words on a plaque, mounted in the narthex: "This is God's House. Be welcome to this House, whosoever you are — whether of this Household or of another way, or wanderers or deserters — be welcome here. But you who are of the Household, pray for us now, for us and for all sinners here or departed, that mercy draws us all one little pace nearer to Love's unveiled and dazzling face."

As we entered on that late winter afternoon, we found the light was dim and the room was small. And yet we felt a sort of momentous presence. My friend and I stood, finally knelt, and simply stayed put for over forty minutes in this tiny chapel. It was one of the times in my life that I felt personally closest to God — not because of the place, or a feeling that somehow he was physically closer, but because I was finally, fully, and completely quiet. There was no flash of revelation; yet at the same time, there was something more than just a feeling of profound peace and warmth. I was here. God was here. It was a moment reminiscent of leaving town and going out to a hill in the distant countryside to look up at the midnight sky, where I could suddenly see and "feel" the stars. The universe might be endless but, somehow, it was very near as well. Likewise here, I belonged. Things were as they should be. In the same instant, I could know that "It's not all about me" yet also believe that "I'm still important."

Such moments of stillness, leading to understanding, are also what prayer has come to be all about for me — not an asking or waiting for changed outcomes, but a sorting, presentation, and listening for the grace of guidance. Occasionally, a really poignant hymn or a truly insightful sermon on Sunday morning can have that same "stilling then stimulating" effect. These are the places where our encounters with God are the most likely, because we somehow manage to will ourselves to listen. I feel the need to do more of this listening as I get older.

If faith, then, involves loving and listening for God in all of life's situations — sometimes large, usually small, just like the quality of all other moments in our lives — then losing faith probably works the same way. Certainly my father thought so. That's why he so strongly shared the view expressed in *Fear and Trembling* and *The Sickness unto Death* by the theologian and fellow Dane Søren Kierkegaard, "that the opposite of sin is not virtue but faith."

The Fourth Lesson

SELF-INDULGENCE
TO THE POINT OF SIN

Jerry Johnson was a lousy disciplinarian. Parental spanking was more than a socially acceptable response to bad behavior when I was growing up. Yet I can recall getting slapped on the rear only twice — once for stealing a package of balloons from the corner store, and once for making fun of a prudish parishioner behind his back (but insufficiently out of range of this aggrieved soul's hearing). The principal impressions I carry from these events are not wounded recollections of fleeting pain, but the decidedly humorous images of my father struggling to work up enough righteousness to administer the stings of punishment.

Even more poignant to me are those memories of times, fortunately few, when my father, far more calmly, suggested disappointment in me over a course of conduct rather than a specific action. I remember, with shame to this day, the shabby way I treated a kid who lived two blocks over, named Jack. Jack and I were the same age, but a year apart in school because Jack had been held back at kindergarten for what would have been readily diagnosed today as a serious learning disability. In those years, however, children like Jack were simply seen as "stupid," and were regularly singled out by others for ridicule. I had befriended Jack and felt bad for him. He was a nice kid, and openly interested in many things, like science fiction television shows and popular music, that intrigued me as well. We were friends, of sorts, when I found friendship convenient. But whenever someone else came along that I thought might be "more cool," my closeness to Jack became a source of embarrassment for me and, in the insecurity of adolescence, I went out of my way to make fun of him, or slight him, to my supposed advantage.

Most days, my parents drove me and others in the neighborhood to school, and Jack was often part of the crowd in the back seat of the car. I remember one morning when my father was driving, and I decided to put on a show of embarrassing Jack in front of others by revealing Jack's secret confession to me of his crush on a classmate. I went to great lengths to describe not only Jack's inner longings, but also the hopelessness of his situation, where someone as "slow" as he was pursuing someone with far greater flash and facility. It was all childish, but still horrible. For my father, who had seen me act unkindly to Jack before but never witnessed a complete performance, it was more than enough. As he let us all out of the car that morning, he asked me to stay behind. Then he said: "What you are doing to that boy is wrong. It is hurtful to him, and it's beneath you to treat him or anybody like that. I don't want you to be this way. In fact, I don't want

71

to see you ever again be that kind of person. I just don't know you when you're like that to another human being."

Those words hit harder than any slap. They hurt all the more because they were so fully justified. They stayed with me. Certainly, I tried to do better by Jack, simply to avoid their recurrence.

My father could well have added to his rebuke (which fortunately, he didn't that day), "And God doesn't want to see you ever again be that kind of person either." Because his stance with me that day reflected my father's theological, as well as his parental, convictions:

> Sin is being less, doing less than God intended us to be and do. If a man wrongs, if he sins against a friend, the actual deed is not what matters most. The deed might be such as would pass unnoticed by most persons. The real pain which both he and his friend feel is due not to the wrong done, but to the fact that the friendship has been broken and betrayed. Sin is more to be described in what I am than in what I do. In fact, I think we should speak of sin in the singular rather than the plural. If I were to rewrite the Apostles' Creed, I would say, "I believe in the forgiveness of sin," not "sins."

My father proposed that, since people are inherently subject to the selfishness that has sometimes been called "original sin," individual wrong actions usually do not reach the bar of theological significance until they wade into the deeper waters of darkness and isolation.

I can see the truth of this in counseling situations. In dealing with problems of parent and child, husband and wife, employer and employee, I tell people that they must try to get beyond looking at just the actual complaint. Parents, dealing with a child who is rebellious and staying out too late, think they simply need to set a curfew, and then the problem is solved. In an argument over money, a frustrated wife says to her husband that if he would just learn how to budget, the problem will be solved. An employer, frustrated by an employee who never shows up to work on time, insists on a sign-in sheet to document the employee's conduct. But these are all actions that treat the symptoms, rather than the deeper problem, the very relationship between parent and child, husband and wife, or employer and employee. When the relationships are right, the problems are usually solved.

Thus, my father concluded: "So with sin. Sin is being less, doing less, than God intended us to be and do. Murder, stealing, lust, infidelity, negligence, drunkenness, laziness, lying, cheating — these are only the symptoms of sin. The antidote for these is not trying to be good. The antidote is a new relationship to God."

I did not conclude from all this that, somehow, my father was denying the many actions that are in themselves grievous and profoundly wrong, or that he saw every misdeed, no matter how serious, as an occasion for therapeutic counseling or redirection. Still, I have found over the years that, when it comes to bad deeds, my personal chemistry tips more toward the Old Testament yearning for judgment, while my father always manifested more resonance with the New Testament teachings of God's grace. In his approach to life, my father had more optimism in his DNA than I have usually managed to find in mine — but of course, I'm the one in the family who ended up going to law school.

My father's notion of sin as a defaulted relationship, rather than an accumulation of foul play, missteps, and bad deeds to be toted up and judged by God at a later time, had other implications that continue to provide me important guidance. While, again, he could readily recognize the depravity in someone who committed murder or some "big" heinous crime, the pattern of sin he observed in most people was far more mundane — so mundane, in fact, that it could often be missed or rationalized away by the transgressor. He called these minor sins and small breaches in the relationship of faith the "little foxes," after a phrase in Song of Solomon 2:15:

"Catch us the foxes,
    the little foxes,
that ruin the vineyards —
    for our vineyards are in blossom."

As my father wrote, "If you have a life, it is not the great sin and the great wrong that so often destroy it, but the host of little sins that burrow in and sap our spirit and warp our vision. We pay a great deal of attention to the lion-like evils that roar and pounce upon us, and not enough to the little sly evils that finally gain entrance and ruin us from within. Catch the little foxes."

We see this "death by a thousand cuts" of life's essential

relationships in many people we know. I have a business colleague with whom I have worked in many sensitive matters over the years. I'm sure he would readily describe himself as a "good person," someone who brings his many years of business experience to the challenges of starting and sustaining smaller companies and helping promising ideas find investment. And in many ways, I would describe him as a good person too. He's kind, and he's reliable at keeping confidences and often provides seasoned, sensible advice. But when it comes to certain things, especially money, he has a broad moral blind spot. He is always trying to find ways to get paid for giving his advice, even though the people we work with are the scientific equivalent of "starving artists" who rarely can afford to pay for the help they need. Of course, it's no sin to want to be compensated for honest work. But sometimes I have watched my friend accept a director's seat, or insist upon a consulting fee, or request some other sort of lucrative arrangement, all behind the scenes, and then participate in investment decisions as if he were a neutral third party. He justifies this type of action — a genuine conflict of interest, at the very least — as "the way the world works." I have seen him in travel situations claim some special privilege and push himself past all other travelers in line in the drive to be served first. Here again, rudeness is not a cardinal sin, but depending upon the circumstances, it can be grounds for a pretty good fight. And I have seen him insist on someone steering a business opportunity to a family member or relative, or even claim a business deduction on his taxes for truly personal travel. Most of these "sins" are truly little foxes. Yet, they not only add up, but they also change my view of where my friend really stands on life. In fact, these actions change where he stands as well. I'm pretty sure that whatever the situation, whenever the question arises, he will seek to further his own advantage, at the expense of others, above all else. He is not ashamed to let others see this part of his character. Selfishness — sinfulness, breaking faith — is just the way of the world, in his view. The result is that he puts not weight, but distance, into his relationship with me and with other people. And so, I think, he puts real distance into his relationship with God.

Some "little foxes" can be entertaining, as well as alienating. One of them — cynicism — has much the same effect, even though most of us don't think of sharp, cynical (and often very funny) comments as being particularly wicked, unless they are intended to hurt someone else. And of course, that is sometimes the case. But the "sin in cynicism" to me is its deadening effect on hope, its worldly certainty — to the point of sharp observation — that life is out of control, that everyone is in it for himself or herself, that the only way to avoid disappointment is to give up being naive. We live in an era of wickedly clever and highly observant one-line jokes, of late-night comedians and entire cable networks that specialize in scrutinizing the news of the day, or the foibles of people (usually, politicians or celebrities or, ideally, both) through the lens of cynical limits, and getting us to laugh at some variation of the theme "How could they believe that?" or "What were they thinking?" or "Could anyone really anticipate that people would act like that?" It's good comedy, and undoubtedly great for ratings and advertising. But the subtext within this cynical content is, "Come on, this is all there is — wise up, or look stupid. And if you persist in your misplaced hope, we're going to call you out on it."

In such a setting, belief in anything — traditional moral values, patriotism, the possibility that banks or insurance companies have good intentions, the ability of any political candidate to bring true change — looks simpleminded and misguided. It leaves the hopeful speaker wide open to ridicule. Again, the message is intended to be expressed as funny, even though it's often rooted in arrogance and in fact represents its own form of naivete: "Get over hoping for something, or someone, better. This is all there is, this is all there ever has been or ever will be, and you're foolish to believe that things could be different." We define the universe with a small, manageable footprint — and within this zone, human intellect (or at least our own intellect) can rule and not be fooled. But it's hard to dream from this perspective. It's also hard to believe in things like a compassionate universe, a loving God, a sacrificial Christ — or the possibility of things unseen that may be better than what's in front of us. I laugh at cynical jokes, and I appreciate their cleverness. At the same time, it seems to me that we run the risk of deadening some of our key faculties — hope, as well as faith — if we succumb to the cynicism of the day.

As I continue to learn the ways of the workplace, I have come to see sin as something even more ordinary, in our world today, than a lifetime of many small misplaced deeds collectively tolling the limits of our larger faith. I have also come to see sin as settling for a lesser relationship with God, and with other people, through our pursuit of a pattern of "living small" through endless clutter, checklists, and multitasking. My father actually preached on this topic, though less as a component of sin, and more as something that simply got in the way of our essential mission when we are so "busy here and there." As he preached in a sermon long ago, "In 1 Kings 20:40, there is a sentence much to the point here. It concerns a man who was entrusted with watching a captive taken in battle in order that the captive did not escape. But the captive did escape, and when the guard was asked to explain it, his answer was 'Lo, and while thy servant was busy here and there, he was gone.' The guard was so busy doing other and lesser things that he forgot his main task, which was to guard the man."

The Reverend Johnson then went on to ask, in this old sermon delivered well before the age of laptop computers, video games, and smart phones, "Isn't this true of many of us who are so busy? So busy, so hurried, so occupied that the important things are sometimes gone before we know it? Busy here and there, and the visions depart, the dreams disappear, the ideals vanish? Busy here and there, and we even lose sight of God?"

I recall making fun of this sermon topic, which I felt was far too obvious for my father to try to reinforce with his congregation. Who didn't get the point that you had to "stop and smell the roses" once in a while, and avoid getting caught up in the noise of everyday life? Yet I see today that his message was in keeping with his larger view of faith as a relationship: that multitaskers and frenetic checklist-doers have a difficult time keeping the important relationships in life in focus — starting with their faith relationship with God. And even more, I see that it is indeed possible to have whole lives, or portions of lives, composed either of mind-numbing routines or equally deadening "small stuff." In fact, I'm pretty sure we often seek out this distraction by detail in an effort to make our lives so filled with events that we can affirm that, after all, we must be important, simply because we are so busy.

I look back at my many years in legal practice, moving from client to client, deal to deal, balancing calendars and conflicts. I realize how much energy, and often, joy, I found simply in being caught up in so many things at once. There's nothing wrong, of course, with living this way, at least if some measure of balance is added in. But my hectic schedule then — and to be honest, now as well, as I add ever more e-mail messages and telephone calls to the routine of a newer workplace — could allow me to go on for days, months, or whole years without really stopping and reflecting on what I was doing, or why I was doing it. I found (and find) meaning in movement, and the more, the better.

When we get caught up like this, it's hard to have time for the relationships that count — relationships with spouses, children, and certainly, God. And it's also surprisingly hard to focus our "busy-ness" on one or two pursuits that matter most, to choose and then to act in a sustained way, when it's the sheer pace of activity, back and forth, that so captivates us. We live in a world of multiple "windows," where many small things can seemingly be accomplished at once. Sometimes it's just very difficult to concentrate on the fewer, bigger things, those relationships that truly should be our business.

Sin for my father represented distance from God, because it also represented distance from other people. In my father's view, sin started with the natural, constant, insistent, but erroneous human belief that "it's all about me." Left to our own devices, we can do a pretty sad job of proceeding through life without real connection to the people and places — the community of saints and sinners — that place our true selves into creation's rightful context. Thus blinded, we are likewise oblivious to our rightful context in a relationship of faith with God. My father found his vocation in addressing sin in this essential form, this lack of living richly and faithfully, that keeps us from seeing and participating in what life is meant to be all about.

But evil was another consideration entirely. For my father, sin could be overcome, or at least forgiven, because it could be understood. Sin was, after all, the way of the world of people, the inevitable consequence of the drive within all of us, in the beginning and at the end, to be out for ourselves. Evil, however, made no sense to him, since in his view evil attached much less to the corrupt conduct of people and far more to the fundamental flaws of creation itself. Questions of sin led my father to address human conduct; questions of evil led him into direct confrontation with God. How could the Father who created this world be fully loving when so much evil just seemed to be built into it? It was in our discussions of this problem, the problem of pain, that I saw my father wrestle most with his faith. And it was in such discussions of his faith that I found, as anticipated, the greatest challenges to my own.

The Fifth Lesson

RIDDLED BY EVIL

E ven a struggle feels better when it's shared. One of the best things about my religious correspondence with my father was the openness he brought to discussions of his theological anxieties as well as his hopes. In seeking to come to terms with my own religious challenges, it helped to see my father so unapologetically seeking to do the same with his. In most areas, and for most questions, he had answers. But as I noted earlier, when it came to explanations for how a loving God could create a world with so much suffering and evil in it, my father readily confessed to drawing a blank. "Why does evil exist in the first place? This topic is such a stumbling block to faith for me. Perhaps I am focusing too intently on it; but it's only honest, and very much in the spirit of these letters, for me to describe the reasons this question of evil must be faced squarely, even if it is a question that, in the end, cannot be fully answered."

From the start of his ministry, my father categorically rejected easy, if disturbing, rejoinders to this question of suffering. His impatience extended to any pious suggestion that we suffer because God wills it, or because God is testing us, or because our suffering is somehow all some surprisingly wonderful part of "God's plan" for us that will be revealed in a rich and righteous afterlife. He believed that the God of grace was not a God who played games with people's lives or, for that matter, a God that planned out every step and every choice of our day-to-day existence. Evil for my father was simply a basic fact, and a basic problem for God and man to face alike.

Within that problem, he did distinguish between what he thought could be characterized as the evil directly caused by human action and the pain arising from forces seemingly beyond our control. ("Did you ever wonder, by the way, why we call an earthquake, flood, or some other natural disaster an 'act of God'? Even insurance companies, it seems, have a theology.") He also allowed that our freedom to choose good or evil, as God's creation, comes with certain risks, and perhaps even "means that God is more intent on our freedom than on our security, and is more interested in our growth than our safety."

But he never invested much intellectual energy in trying to create a detailed framework for rational discussion of evil's components and finer points, simply because he doubted that any meaningful explanation was even possible:

Of course, of course, I understand that evil or wrong needs to be one of the choices we are free to make, starting with Adam in the Garden of Eden. Yet my problem remains. It's a problem that comes with creation itself, with the natural evil that exists, with the cruelty inherent in wind and weather, the deadly toll of time, the frailty of our bodies. To say this is a fallen world due to humankind's rebellion and sin may explain some diseases and deaths, accidents and war, pestilence and starvation. But why are children of good and normal parents born disabled? Why do we have floods, and droughts? A cyclone in Bangladesh kills 140,000 poor and innocent people and leaves millions more homeless. Is this catastrophe the hand of God?

It worried him. And his troubling question was "How can a good and loving Father permit a world so full of disaster and pain and sorrow? Christ may be the final answer, but why the question exists in the first place is, for me, an everlasting mystery."

In looking back over our correspondence now, and even more in rereading some of my father's later sermons and devotional meditations, I am struck by the size of this "problem of pain" for him. Over the course of our letters, he returned to it repeatedly; he confessed that this issue continued to place him in fundamental conflicts of the highest order. "The older I get, and the more I continue in my ministry, the more doubtful I am that there are any easy answers to the question of why God's world is such an imperfect world, and the more impatient I become with those who claim that those easy answers exist. Certainly, God and I have argued over the whole subject for years. He has made me accept my limitations, and I do, but not very graciously, I fear."

At the time of our letter exchange, I didn't really have much to say in response. In truth, his words of distress did not resonate with me as the biggest impediment to my own beliefs, or my own relationship of faith. Looking back now, though, given how much I identified with everything else my father had to say in this correspondence, it strikes me as curious that such a highly charged topic for him did not engage me more.

Certainly, even then, I found the question of why there is so much suffering in God's "perfect" world to be troubling and very definitely worth asking for real answers. I had already encountered the book of Job in a college literature class, and had been required to explicate the dramatic text of this Old Testament story of one of God's most ancient, faithful, and famously tormented sufferers. In the account, Job, for reasons he can never understand, is literally forced to face the tortures of the damned. He does occasionally question his suffering. And in admittedly poetic imagery (Job 38:2-7; 40:8), here is what Job gets in return:

"Who is this that darkens counsel by words without
     knowledge?
Gird up your loins like a man,
     I will question you, and you shall declare to me.
Where were you when I laid the foundation of the earth?
     Tell me, if you have understanding.
Who determined its measurements — surely you know!
     Or who stretched the line upon it?
On what were its bases sunk,
     or who laid its cornerstone

when the morning stars sang together
and all the heavenly beings shouted for joy? . . .
Will you even put me in the wrong?
Will you condemn me that you may be justified?"

I intensely disliked this story, and its implications, from
the very first time I read it. Certainly, I agreed with my father's own reading and reaction to Job's account: "This story
seems to me an easy way out when it says we need to take our
universe, our physical environment, as a given and go on
from there, that God's ways are not men's ways. Well, yes —
but they ought to be *better* than men's ways."

But even more, the Old Testament God of this story
struck me as far more aloof, and considerably more arrogant,
than the God of the New Testament who sends Christ in
search of the ultimate relationship of faith, trust, and love
with his creation. It's not much of a relationship when the
parent, as in Job's case, says essentially, "I'm in charge. Don't
question me. I'll tell you what to do." That's a response on par
with "Take your medicine" or "Father knows best" — it's
hard to feel very warm or open toward someone or something that takes such an approach. But that's not the God of
the New Testament. The God of the Gospel accounts would
want us to ask; or at least, through Christ, it seems he would
understand our need to do so.

So the discussion is valid. And if my father and I were to
engage in it today, I suspect I would have four points to make
to him as a more faithful correspondent.

First, I now think it is worth trying to distinguish between
the "evil of chaos" of a rough and rugged world into which

we're born, and the "evil of suffering" that mankind seems uniquely good in bestowing upon itself and that is, indeed, one of the unfortunate consequences of the freedom we enjoy as God's creation. It's worth doing this because it ends up making us feel lots better about God, even if we inevitably also end up feeling a lot worse about people.

My father had little patience with dwelling upon this distinction in his search for the larger point of what he perceived as God's overall responsibility for a flawed creation. In part, that was perhaps an easier leap for him to make because of his general approach to human evil as being "nondramatic," more a product of selfishness and pettiness than spectacular examples of just downright wickedness. It's not that he didn't believe in the latter, but he saw evil's more common form less as some "big force" of darkness and more as primarily the millions of smaller, self-serving, self-asserting things we do to distance ourselves from those that matter, starting with God and extending to fundamental relationships across the spectrum of life. I share this view to a great extent, and find it helpful in defining life's essential values, as well as the foundations of my own faith.

Yet perhaps, unlike my father, I find true "big evil" — if not an objective force in its own right — to be an unmistakable and often violent presence that ranges far beyond normal human selfishness (and sin) but still comes far more frequently from people than from God. This observation may hold true for me because I am graced with a less sunny outlook on life than Jerry Johnson brought to it. Or it may arise from the fact that we live in a world of instant and intensive media, of the glaring eye of the video lens, the cell phone camera, and the webcam on each and every act of human cruelty and shortcoming.

Perhaps we are simply better at seeing and less adept at escaping true evil than ever before. My father's views were formed in a world that really couldn't conceive of the plotting of Osama bin Laden that brought the horrors of 9/11, or the systemic cruelty of Pol Pot, or the paranoid delusions of Timothy McVeigh. The world of my father's youth didn't see, until it was almost too late, the evil of an Adolf Hitler — or a Josef Stalin. Though I'm convinced that insanely wicked incidents like the Columbine High School killings or the Fort Hood massacre are not new to human experience, their thorough and immediately accessible documentation is unprecedented. We are crowded, nearly daily, with unmistakable and vivid video evidence of the depravity of others, and the suffering we can inflict upon each other. Understanding the shape, the depth, and the extent of evil may be one of the greatest benefits of our "instantly linked" culture — and, of course, one of its largest curses.

Some in my father's generation indeed realized that the depth and extent of evil in the world were so difficult to comprehend that it was often easier simply not to see. That is the very reason that the Allied conquerors of Hitler's Europe, in 1945, determined from the first time they set foot within them to preserve the gruesome evidence of designed systems of widespread human torture at the newly liberated Nazi concentration camps. Thus, nearly half a century later, when I was part of a business delegation to visit the notorious Auschwitz concentration camp in Poland, I could still see the enormous piles — rooms full — of suitcases, clothes, eyeglasses, and false teeth assembled by the Nazis from those who entered and would never depart the camp, artifacts preserved by the conquering Allies. I could still walk into the barracks where camp residents lived like livestock, and visit the ovens and gas chambers where they were slaughtered the same way. Most vivid to me was the planning map display of the Nazi-dominated European system of rail connections that brought Jews from every corner of western, central, and eastern Europe right to the concentration camp at Auschwitz, planned and scheduled in meticulous detail. More than anything else I saw, here was evidence of evil not as the passionate choice made in a moment of blinding rage, but as the systematic, shared, deliberate drawing out of a network of suffering by those who professed to be both enlightened and Christian, day after day, month after month. Something large and misshapen and widely shared was at work in the Nazi culture. Despite living through this period, my father somehow never seemed to truly know this evil, or to see evidence of it.

I'm pretty sure that even the optimistic Jerry Johnson might have had an altered view of human nature if he had witnessed, at an earlier stage in his life's journey, some of the many images that have made up my formative years — not to mention my teenaged daughter's. They are images that continue to confirm my suspicion that evil, while perhaps not amounting to a truly separate force or presence, is nevertheless a deep and dark river of ever-present possibility in this world, just waiting for humans to jump in.

So, given my conviction that human evil takes larger shape and more widespread form than my father customarily assumed, my second point to him would be that the responsibility for what he saw as evil in this world indeed often belongs more to people than to God. Wars, terrorist attacks, and genocide are all clear examples of mass destruction and human suffering brought about by evil choices on a monstrous — but still human — scale. Many who suffer and die in these events have committed no wrong action beyond literally being, or residing, at the wrong place at the wrong time in history. Still, the evil and devastation that are caused appear to be properly allocated to the human, rather than the divine, side of the ledger. These are lives damaged or lost because of the actions and wrong choices of people, and not some heavenly force. Climate change and species extinction are phenomena whose ultimate impacts are "natural" but, in today's world, whose principal causes more often than not come straight from us.

And it is increasingly clear that even some of the suffering brought about by seeming "acts of God" is often aggravated — to the point of near causality — by the actions or inactions of people. The massive destruction, death, and dislocation caused by Hurricane Katrina in 2005 had their origin in an enormous hurricane. Katrina realized its deadly potential, however, through the actions and inactions of a city, state, and nation that were famously unprepared to anticipate, and then to deal with, such a disaster. Today, beyond the immediate tragedy of death and destruction brought by an epic combination of earthquake and tsunami in early 2011, the people of Japan (and the world) face what is arguably an even greater, ongoing peril: critical damage — including multiple meltdowns — set in motion by the tsunami at several nuclear reactors, inadequately prepared and unfortunately located in eastern Japan.

Perhaps most striking, two major earthquakes, occurring only a month apart in early 2010, first in Haiti and then in Chile, showed the destructive difference that human actions or inactions can make in times of natural catastrophes. In Haiti, a sudden earthquake immediately offshore brought the collapse of an entire city (and almost of the country's government); the death of over 200,000 people trapped by falling buildings and piles of rubble; and a shocking, sudden legacy of ongoing disease, looting, dislocation, and instability. In Chile, an even more momentous earthquake managed to generate hundreds of times more energy than its Haitian counterpart, hitting with sufficient strength to shift the earth's axis and even shorten the planet's day permanently.

Yet in Chile, the death toll from a quake of such truly biblical proportions, though substantial, was less than 0.4 percent of the Haitian total. The physical destruction to buildings and roads was far less. The reasons for the difference were, of course, not the quake but the human surroundings of its impact: in Chile, strictly enforced building codes ensured that the vast majority of structures were built to withstand, or at least lessen, the shock of such a quake. The Chilean poverty rate is also far lower, and so people were not living literally on top of one another in cinder-block shanties of the type obliterated in the Haitian quake. The Chilean government was also better prepared to act, and did so, while in Haiti, precious hours were lost with no one in charge of recovery. As Eben Harrell summarized this tale of two earthquake cities in a March 15, 2010, essay in *Time* magazine,

"When the Earth Moves": "There is a lesson in this. . . . To walk through Chile's gleaming and unbroken capital is to learn that although earthquakes, when coupled with dire poverty, can do terrible harm, we have the capacity to mitigate it. . . . When things are broken, Chile reminds us, they can be fixed."

We may have been placed by God in a challenging world shaped by destructive forces beyond our control. But we can often overcome those forces, or at least come to terms with them. Just as often, through our own actions or inactions, we can also make the outcomes of those basic forces far, far worse.

This observation brings me to my third point: modern science shows us an earth that appears to be a small and remarkable, life-sustaining chip of an incomprehensibly larger universe created by divine but explosive forces that continue to expand and shape it. I'm not sure my father would have agreed.

> The Bible says that God looked out upon his creation and saw that it was good. But I cannot believe that God, if he were capable of a perfect creation, would build a universe that was so obviously imperfect. So that leaves us two, truly unsatisfactory alternatives: either God was limited in his ability to create, and created an imperfect world; or else this is the best possible kind of world and God has hidden and mysterious reasons of his own — reasons he has not shared with us — for creating a world that contains so much suffering and pain. That second alternative doesn't speak well for the love in our relationship.

Actually, maybe it does, given what we know about the rest of creation, in which we may play a small part, but also in which there is clearly much more going on that we cannot begin to comprehend. Every year we gain further insight into just how big, how unknown, and how unknowable (at least, within a million light-years) the universe really is. We get better and better glimpses of the forces at work in flattening, driving, and spreading a universe that, incomprehensibly, hasn't stopped growing and appears to have something else into which it is expanding. Think about that: What does a universe expand into? How can those words ever begin to make sense? More to the immediate point, and a bit closer to planet Earth, given the true chaos that surrounds us and what we know today to be a churning series of galaxies of black holes and exploding stars and supernovas, it's remarkable that the basic rhythm of days and events in this part of the universe — on planet Earth — is as tranquil as it usually is. When we consider the powerful forces at work nearly everywhere else, I at least am impressed that the truly natural disasters that plague us are neither far worse nor far more frequent.

In saying this, I don't seek to deny the truth of my father's conviction that people have been placed in an often dangerous and unstable world. But I wonder if we shouldn't simply seek to place this conviction in the larger context of the incomprehensible, explosive dynamism and chaotic energy that appear to be God's building blocks for the universe itself, ones that appear to have been used in astonishingly livable moderation when it comes to constructing the fabric of life on this planet.

Part of what also should make our world-created-from-

chaos even more livable is God's best creation — us. We have
been blessed with sufficient skill and sense, and the capacity
to develop even more of it, to address many circumstances
that could otherwise be disastrous. I need only be reminded
that, in the course of my lifetime, polio has been nearly eradi-
cated in the developed world; AIDS has been introduced,
discovered, and now treated as a chronic disease rather than a
death sentence; and antibiotics fight infections that were invariably fatal less than a century ago. I work every day with
scientists and entrepreneurs and investors determined to
find, prove, and produce vaccines for cancer, biologic drugs
to treat macular degeneration, and real remedies for the tragedy of Alzheimer's disease and dementia (baby boomers are
placing special emphasis on the various diseases of aging as
chronology makes the stakes for solutions more personal and
hence more urgent).

My father might well have agreed that a big part of our
purpose in life should be working to make real improvements
in where we are and how we live. After all, he once allowed
that it was probably too early to assess the process of creation
because it was simply unfinished:

> God has given us the essential ingredients of life and mat-
> ter, but creation is an ongoing thing. And in this contin-
> uing labor of creation, God insists that people join with
> him. Imagine! God calls us to share as partners in this un-
> believable and overwhelming plan to bring, as Paul says
> in his letter to the Ephesians, "Everything together with
> Christ as head." Meanwhile, ours remains an adolescent
> world, undergoing the pain and torment, the frustration

and agony of maturing. Maybe, just maybe, it's true that we will share in the work and then share in the glory when God's will is finally done, on earth as it is in heaven.

The older I get, and the more I see what we can do, even with limited knowledge, the more I believe that Jerry Johnson got this point exactly right. My regret is that he didn't see how much this realization could help in removing some of the sting he felt from the problem of pain in God's world.

My fourth and final comment to my father would be a confession: that when it comes to being troubled by why things are the way they are, and why creation is what it is, my biggest challenge turns out to be not the general problem of good versus evil but the very particular, and highly personal, reality of life versus death. If God loves us so much that he would sacrifice his authority, his distance, and ultimately his own Son and self for our salvation, why doesn't he want to keep us around for eternity, just as we are, hopefully subject to some considerable improvement over the years? Why does this relationship he seeks from us ultimately have to end — or certainly, appear to end — in what is so often a period of decline, pain, disease, and death? Why is God's timeless love so limited for us in this world by time?

This question of suffering and death has plagued me from my earliest thinking moments. I can recall being very young, perhaps five or six years old, enjoying the warmth of a road trip on a summer evening and gazing out the rear window of our family car. As I looked up at the sky and saw the real beauty of the fading light and approaching evening, I found myself suddenly, somehow, contemplating . . . not being around to look up at the sky at all. I could almost feel nothingness. It was terrifying to me then, and very vivid, very cold. And I can still conjure this vision, this feeling, when I allow my mind to wander back to that jumping-off point. It baffles and discourages me. To put so much into shaping a life, relationships with God and with others, working, changing, hopefully growing — and then, often at a time the world deems too early, everything in this life comes to an end. In a loving universe where a person has been created and then developed over the course of a lifetime (however much time that may be), such a fate seems terribly unfair.

The Christian has an answer, and a really good one, for this question. That answer, of course, is that because Jesus literally shared our pain and faced and then triumphed over death, we do not truly die after all. Instead, we continue in eternal, resurrected life with God. It is a great answer, one that in essence moves beyond the question and seeks to provide assurance that death is not the end. But even if we can believe in this message, can we truly take full comfort in it? Even if we are ultimately redeemed, the fact remains that death, and the converging causes of it, generally produce real anxiety and substantial mental — and usually physical — suffering in its inevitable progression. Our soul may be saved, but our body (and much of our mind) is captive to a process that makes it hard for some of us to appreciate that message at the most basic level.

We are hardwired to resist death. Even Christ on the cross felt the sharpness of this pain and, seemingly, a fair degree of doubt ("'Eloi, Eloi, lema sabachthani?' which means, 'My God, my God, why have you forsaken me?'" [Mark 15:34]).

Death does matter. It's difficult, often painful, and even more often scary. Why are we, as God's beloved creation, forced to pass — and pass through — it?

Interesting to me now, and not a little remarkable, is that in all his letters to me and the many more sermons my father authored on the questions of suffering, evil, and pain, there is no teaching — no sermon, no letter — I can find that really addresses this question of why we need to die. Surely, he heard this question from anxious parishioners, and probably far more frequently than he heard the more "cosmic" question of why there is so much pain and suffering integrated into the fabric of creation. Yet, my father never preached on it; he never even wrote about it directly. As one who watched him die, I think I know the answer to my own question: he didn't like death, but he pretty clearly didn't much fear it either. He was eager to get on to the next phase of what he believed, with ultimate confidence, was his eternal life. That last lesson from him was, for me, definitely the hardest.

The Sixth Lesson

NOT IMMORTAL BUT ETERNAL

Beyond the confines of my family, my first really serious discussion of religion concerned the subject of eternal life. I was in college, and the incident occurred early on, during the months of my earnest exchange of letters with my father. I had gone into town to get that rarest of all self-improvements for any college student at that time — a haircut. I visited a small barbershop (one that still had one of those touching, twirling blue and white poles outside), run by two Italian brothers. Like all barbers, they liked to talk, but their work was good and the price was reasonable. When I went in, I noticed that only one of the two barber brothers was there. I asked him about business, of course, and where his brother was. That innocuous question tipped off a troubling conversation.

My barber told me that he and his brother had taken turns working because business had not been good enough in recent months (this was, after all, the 1970s, when all fashions

97

were essentially ridiculous and all hair was unmanageably long) to support them both. During the winter, his brother had generally been the one in the shop, but he had worked there on Wednesdays. Plus he had put in ten hours a day at the post office. He had had a reason for multiple jobs, he said, but that reason was gone now.

It was a loaded question, but I asked it. Why?

There was a long silence — long, at least, for a barber shop. He told me he had been working in the post office so he could send his son to college. He had three children, and had always seen a full education as one of the best parts of the American dream. As immigrants, he and his brother had never had much education themselves, and had always felt trapped in their business. He wanted it different for his kids. It didn't work out that way for the first two. Neither one was interested in college. But, he said, at least he had given them a good home and they were both now pretty happy in their own work. Then there was his third child, a boy. He had been "the scholar of the family." He was a pretty good student. And captain of the track team. "Everybody loved him." He had gotten offers from three colleges within the state. His father was overjoyed. But he didn't want his son to know. He didn't want his son to get "the big head" and go off and spend a lot of money on a car or some similarly expensive distraction and then not be able to go to college. So on the side, without telling his son, the father had taken another job. He had planned to surprise his son and give him the money at graduation. Meanwhile, he told his boy to hang onto his money. He had him look into loans and jobs. He wanted to impress upon his son what a big — and expensive — event his college education would be. But he was a proud father. And the father would do well by his child.

"Everybody loved him."

There was another of those pauses in the conversation. Then the barber said that two months before, his son's high school had held one of the year's biggest track meets. His son had had a cold for a few days before, but it was nothing serious. He would be up for his race. "The whole team was counting on him."

His son ran in the race. But he never finished it. From his first-place lead in the race, the boy suddenly fell back and then, apparently, just fell over. "My boy was dead." Dead at the age of eighteen, from acute pneumonia. Dead without ever knowing his father's surprise.

The barber's voice was breaking now. "My wife, it's the hardest on her. She can't ever talk about it, so I have no one to discuss it with." Then I realized that for every day for over a month, this man had been standing over his customers going through the agony of that same story. His customers were the only ones who would listen.

He was not only grieving the loss of "my special son." He was guilty. The boy had resented his father's hard-nosed attitude toward work and money, and told him so. But the father had gone firmly on, happily building up to the big surprise that would never come. And then he hadn't noticed the boy was ill. "He was always so strong. If only I'd realized he wasn't well. He didn't have to die. One of his friends told me later he'd taken Danny up to look at the University of Massachusetts and my boy slept all the way. Why didn't he know something was wrong?"

He turned my chair around to show me his work in the mirror.

"But they loved him. They were all there. The whole school was at his funeral. The principal, he said over and over again, what a loss. There were tears in their eyes — in all their eyes." There were tears in his eyes too.

Not just to be sad, but guilty. All the rest of his life. To feel his son died despising him and not knowing his love. That was what really ripped me apart. And the father then said, "But I figure one thing, this I can be sure of. Life goes on. It doesn't all end here. I'll be able to be with him someday and then he'll know. He knows now. But then I'll be able to tell him myself. Father to son."

He asked, "You do believe in eternal life, don't you?"

I have always been grateful that at that moment, somehow, I was able to summon the one best word I could muster in response.

"Yes," I said. "Yes, I do."

Soon after this incident I shared the details with my father in one of my letters home. I requested a better understanding of just what I was affirming when I answered that mourning barber's question the way I did. My father had much to say in response.

He opened by making clear the depth of his conviction that the resurrection of Christ was a historical event. His insistence on this matter was somewhat surprising to me, because my father was not one to stress the factual truth of many of the reported miracles in the Bible, preferring to see them as perhaps more literary than literal in making some larger point about Christ's divinity or God's concern for his creation. But he felt the resurrection story had been, indeed, a large, a real, and even, to many, a troubling event.

I tell my parishioners: clearly, something happened that had never happened before, following Christ's death on the cross and the placement of his body in the tomb. Take the apostles, as an example. All of a sudden, this often meandering group of confused and limited souls became like men possessed. They were filled with the glory of something beyond the world. They braved wind and storm, the arena and martyrdom. Only something they saw and experienced, only something they believed to be the truth could make them act like that. They simply knew that Jesus was alive and with them, that he had risen from the dead. And that knowledge turned cowards into heroic men, and disbelievers into preachers of the truth.

Thus, my father concluded: "The details of time's disruption, the stories of transformed conduct, the stunning failure of anxious authorities to produce Jesus' body (a step that would surely have ended, forever, the apostles' insistence that Jesus still lived), and the multiple accounts of Christ's appearances to gatherings of believers. All these things simply defy conventional or cynical explanation. Conceiving of the resurrection is inevitably hard; but the basis for believing it is indisputably present." For him, this "resurrection of the body" carried an important theological as well as historical context. Indeed, my father's further explanation made clearer to me his reasons for according such great weight to the Gospel accounts of Christ's physical resurrection. Typical for him, that explanation involved a bit of scholarship: "The New Testament writers wanted to make clear that the eternal life opened by Christ was very different from the classical concept of immortality. Immortality is a Greek, rather than a Judeo-Christian, idea. The Greeks believed that man was born with an immortal soul, one that was inherently divine and not subject to corruption. The soul was something essentially good, housed in a body which was evil. At death, the immortal soul escaped from the prison of mortal flesh and blood and returned to its source."

Christians, on the other hand, see that all of man — very definitely, including the soul — is subject to sin and corruption. And so, my father concluded, the resurrection was truly redemptive because it was not only a miraculous event, but also a complete one.

New Testament writers did not have the psychological and anthropological concepts, or words to express them, that we use so commonly today. To the biblical writer, "the body" was the "total man" — body, mind, and soul. Had the authors of the Gospels been writing today, they probably would have spoken of the "resurrection of the personality" — of the "whole person." The message they were so urgently seeking to deliver in the accounts of Christ's resurrection was that the essential person lives on. The total man continues after death as a uniquely distinctive individual, not just as a disembodied spirit.

And then, though it was a letter to his son, vocational habit took over — he stopped teaching and started preaching: "And this means that, throughout eternity, in whatever form our eternal presence may take, we shall still recognize each other. I shall be I, and you will be you. I will know you as *you*. You will know me as *me*. We will be with God, but we will not merge with God to become some amorphous form of 'soul.' Heaven will not be some nebulous, misty condition — some place of shades and ghosts. It will be a place of people; a place of reality; a place of life and joy and activity in which we shall have a part."

Now he brought his thinking directly home to me. "I find this very comforting, and I know you will too, since you are concerned that your ego, your mind, your ambitions not end at the moment of death. That is one part of the faith in eternal life that I have, and the part I believe is scriptural. The other part is a little more involved."

As a child, I really liked the idea of divine judgment, probably because of some hidden, hilarious confidence that, given my family's long-standing ties to church and cross, I would inevitably end up on the right side of it. I found it appealing that, like a good book, people's stories in life would come to a conclusion, with some endings happy and some sad, but all richly deserved. It seemed to me to be the fairest way for God to go about ordering things.

Over time, and even as a college student, my romantic notion of godly justice became more complicated. Questions of who and what were "good," and how to tell, became far more complex. Among other things, I grew more sensitive to the seemingly fundamental unfairness in the notion that all people — including the vast majority of the world's population who had never heard much of anything about the supposed good news of the New Testament — would be judged for all time by a single divine standard claimed by one religion. By the time of my collegiate correspondence with my father, I was considerably less eager to contemplate a single "final exam" in life, and certainly far less confident of my ability (or anyone's, for that matter) to pass it. My father was well aware of my struggles in this regard, and so he addressed them with the "more involved" part of his thinking on eternal life.

He started by pointing out that Jesus himself spoke of eternal life as a present fact, rather than some decision to be made in the future: "And this is eternal life, that they may know you, the only true God, and Jesus Christ whom you have sent" (John 17:3). This distinction had etymological and theological import to my father, who proceeded to note that the word Christ used for "eternal" in this verse was the Greek word *ainios*. He explained:

This word *ainios* was used by the Greeks long before the New Testament was written. It had several meanings, but one of its prime definitions was "timeless" or "unending." Eventually, the word was ascribed to the reign of a monarch — just as we might say, "Long live the king." From there, it took on the idea of describing the kind of life the king lived, one that was different from the life of any of his subjects — richer, fuller, happier, more comfortable. And eventually, the Greeks used this word in reference to the gods themselves, denoting a quality of life not possessed by man, a life that transcended time and its attendant evils.

Bringing this lesson forward to the words of the Gospel of John, my father wrote:

So, when the word "eternal" was used in the New Testament, it was to describe the kind of life that God lived, the kind of life that emanated from God. It is a quality of life that belongs only to God; it is the life he can *share* with his people. If you follow this through, you will see that it means that those of us who believe we can have eternal life thus believe that we can share in the life and power and peace of God himself. The important thing is that we are talking here about the *kind* of life, the *quality,* the *essence,* rather than merely an infinitude of time. Every once in a while, I'll hear someone say, "I wouldn't want to live forever." Probably not, if all we are talking about is endless existence. But if we are talking about stepping forward from the vestibule of heaven here on earth and sharing in the very kind of life that God himself lives, that's a different matter.

Over the years since our correspondence, I have continued to think about this explanation of eternal life versus immortality. I have also continued to take comfort in my father's message. It suggests that the relationship we are called upon to form with God is genuinely worthwhile, and does not come to an end, because through grace we do not come to an end. Yet as I have grown considerably older, and now had repeated (and not always welcome) occasion to see in detail the lives of so many others confronting life's opportunities, its challenges, and even death, I am curious whether my father's

concept of eternal life, at least for some, constitutes a blessing
— or a curse. Perhaps heaven and hell are unlikely flip sides of
the same, cosmic coin, where through our actions or inactions in the moment, we essentially get to make the call for
everything that follows.

I find it easiest to think about a question on this scale by
considering a couple of examples. My thoughts run to two
very good but very different men, both lawyers, both friends I
have known and worked with in our community. Sadly, I have
recently been privileged to attend the funerals of each. I recall
the first one, who died last year at a young age, from a sudden
recurrence of cancer he had so confidently believed to be in re-
mission. I spoke with him just a few weeks before his death,
well before he was even aware his cancer had returned. He had
been restless to get on with his life, and to accomplish more
within whatever time he had remaining, which he figured to
be a good many years. It was very clear how much he still
wanted to do in his work, for his young family (through a second marriage) of four children, and for his community, where
he gave endless amounts of time to presiding over the pitched
battles of the local school board. One evening, as I was return-
ing a backlog of office e-mail messages from my home computer, I happened to flip over to the online edition of our local
newspaper, forever multitasking in an effort to get a jump on
the news of the next morning. There, in the breaking head-
lines, was the announcement of the death of a "prominent local school board president." I instantly had a bad feeling. As I
clicked on to the story, my friend's picture came up. I couldn't
believe it — in many ways, I still can't. Neither could his family, his many friends and coworkers, and the community he

left behind. This was a shocking and in every way "premature" death for all of us. Predictably, the turnout for his funeral a few days later was large, sad, and somber. A year later, his death remains a tragedy. But I'm convinced that his great life remains, because it seemed to have all the right stuff to stand not only the test of time but also the test of eternity. Right up to the end, here was someone still "becoming" that person, father, husband, worker, community leader, and even religious believer he had always sought to be. And so for me, he is someone that it is easy — if such a thing can ever be easy — to still *see,* living fully and richly forever, in touch with God and with God's greater creation after having been so fully in touch with what counted right here.

I also think of my second friend. He was just a few years older than my first friend, though considerably more public in his success. His was a career often written about; he was deeply involved in community and political issues, successfully founding and later managing what became a law firm of substantial size and influence. Like my first colleague, he was not much of a churchgoer. He was, however, someone that in today's parlance would definitely qualify as a "thought leader," someone the media frequently sought out for comment on various issues of the day. He was seemingly open and friendly, yet still one of those people you didn't get to know better simply by spending more time with. He had a fixed, public personality — an appealing one, but something of a self-generated one as well. I knew that his relationships with his two older sons were strained. But I didn't know the extent of his detachment from others until his funeral service, where, as it turned out, no one — including his children and colleagues — could think of much that was very warm or very personal, or even especially memorable, to say about him. His sons sought to speak in terms of a father who set high standards and could be described as a model to emulate but never match. Yet the unmistakable image suggested by their words was that of a father who was simply never present, who set expectations for his family that he would have recognized as either unnecessary or unrealistic had he known that family better. Over the course of a thirty-minute series of eulogies, we learned of a life that seemingly knew no limits when it came to public ambition and professional work, but observed early boundaries when it came to personal relationships. There was a strangeness, almost a coldness, about the entire event — one that seemed to emanate from a lack of better content for recollection in any sort of intimate tribute to a man who would still have met nearly every conventional definition of the concept of "good."

Perhaps this man was burdened with inarticulate or ungrateful children. Maybe his true friends had other engagements that kept them from being present. It's always dangerous to draw major conclusions from isolated events, however telling they appear to be. But realizing this might indeed have been a life that could be busily sketched but never richly pictured, I found myself depressed as I departed the service. Certainly, I was sad to lose my friend and colleague. Yet the tragedy here went far deeper. If this memorial service had indeed captured the story of his life on earth, where was the material for what we all hope must be the next chapter in that eternal communion with God? Or, to put it even more bluntly, what did my friend truly bring to the party? What was timeless about a life of sharp deals but shallow relationships? I'm sure the real person, and thus the real answer, was far more wonderfully complex than the accounting I witnessed. But I wonder if it was not also a life likely to be limited in its capacity to move beyond time's boundaries.

The point seems to be that the part of ourselves that is truly "eternal" is the part that's connected to the rest of God's creation — to the world and to other people in this life; to God and to all that heaven may be in life's next installment. If we can't enjoy or be open to others here, how can we be open to God in eternity? What will make heaven "heavenly" for us? My father believed that such observations had true theological validity. As he wrote in his own explanation of all that eternal life might actually demand:

> Through eternity's infinite time, it would seem we continue to become what we were in the process of becoming at the time of death. If the direction of our life is "upward," we have all eternity to follow that upward course, coming closer and closer to the splendor of the presence of God. If the direction of our life is "downward" at the time of death, we have all eternity to move farther and farther away from the presence of God. Looked at in this way, heaven becomes not a reward, not something we earn, but rather a continuation of the life we *choose* to live — and the person we choose to become, or choose not to become — here on earth.

Such a concept of eternal life as forever being what we have been becoming in life on earth is, of course, not particularly original and, again, not always inspiring. The great English writer and theologian C. S. Lewis wrote in his religious fantasy *The Great Divorce* about a visit to a world beyond ours where someone, ill-tempered during life on earth, becomes nothing more than a little ball of pure, evil temper. Lewis looks in on a forever-Napoleon who struts his way pointlessly through eternity to become only a vain rooster-like shadow of a human being.

More recently, the novelist Philip Roth, in his 2008 book *Indignation,* tells the story of a life that goes tragically (if comically) wrong for a young man finding himself, in sudden death, suspended somewhere outside of time and forever nineteen. "Who could have imagined that one would have forever to remember each moment of life down to its tiniest component? . . . As in life, I know only what is, and in death what is turns out to be what was. You are not just shackled to your life while living it, you continue to be stuck with it after you're gone."

Even my father was challenged with some of the implications of his interpretation of eternal life: "My real problem with all this is that there seems to be no 'second chance' beyond this life. I guess I want to hope that God will somehow intervene and make me different from what I am. I realize, according to what we have been talking about, that the choice is my own. But sometimes, I am too weak to choose well."

In my own life, I have become highly attentive to these caveats, and remain grateful that so far, every day — and certain days in particular — has not been my last. This gratitude comes in large measure because I enjoy life as I live it, and with whom I live it now. I feel I have much more to do. But I am also relieved because there are so many days already passed, and so many things I seem to do within each of them, that I truly would not wish to commend to eternity.

Surely, as my father suggests, there is above all some continuing possibility for hope in our relationship with God. And surely while eternal life may start here, and so what we do, or don't do, really does "count" in allowing us to begin to assemble the stuff of eternity, there is still the chance of God's redemption, for our real change — just as there is in any relationship of love. Isn't that the real lesson of the parable of the prodigal son? Isn't that the assurance given to the thief crucified on the cross next to Christ? Of course, even the prodigal son had to realize what was valuable, to lay himself before it and seek it, to be truly open and expect nothing in return, before love and grace could restore him to his rightful place with his father. So did the thief. What I hope such accounts signify is that, mercifully, it is never too late for such realization, and never too late to breathe what remains of life into what must be our essential relationships, both with other people and with God himself.

That is what I hope.

But in the meantime, what I know is that I stand constantly in the midst of selfish, live-for-the-moment prodigal sons (and daughters) who believe, confidently or covertly, that life really is after all just about them, and who have not yet hit the small and shallow bottom of self-obsession. To be honest, they're not just all around me; I'm one of them. Getting older, I find I have judged too much of my own success as a "builder" by the career I have pursued, the money I have made, the reputation I have developed. These are all im-

portant things — but they don't begin to add up to a life cali-
brated to go the distance that my faith suggests. Though I
may now be deep into middle age, I had better get used to the
idea that I can never even consider retirement from the pursuit of what, and who, matters most of all.

The Seventh Lesson

SHOWING UP FOR WORK

W hen I was young, the approach of every summer's school recess made me wonder why I couldn't be granted a similar vacation from attendance at Sunday church services. After all, both routines were about learning, improving myself, making other people (especially my parents) happy. School demanded this sort of discipline only nine months out of every year; as a student, the summer was left just for me. What was it about church that wouldn't give me a similar break, and let me return to duty in the fall? For a preacher's kid, normally expected to show up each Sunday for two long services plus the odious "coffee hour" of polite conversation (and no running through the halls) in between, the question seemed to carry particular merit.

I will confess I often still feel this way about going to church. More than occasionally I act on those feelings. If a long week has just passed, or if travel is in store for the week to come; if I haven't had enough time with my family or I'm feeling unduly stressed and tired; if I convince myself that I just wouldn't "get a lot out of going today," then I can pretty readily sleep in, read the newspaper (for my once-a-week indulgence in turning pages and turning off the computer screen), or watch political and news talk shows. It's all part of a pleasant Sunday morning schedule, more deliberately paced and remarkably free from recriminations for self-indulgence.

But I know I'm missing something. It's not that I'm not going to be a "worse person," or even, most likely, forgo some blazing insight imparted in the morning sermon that will cause me to see and make life's choices more clearly. It's not even about going to church for self-improvement. It's about showing up. It's about affirming that I am part of something larger, part of a community that has made an important choice, part of a group that has much to say and a great deal to do in the world. If I look at it right, I should feel the same way about missing church that I feel about missing work, which, like school, allows vacations but, unlike school, doesn't cease making demands simply because someone's away. Yet I miss church far more often, and with considerably less remorse.

For my father, of course, church was work. And work wasn't always pleasant. "Sometimes, I think that if I have to listen attentively to one more sincere, stupid idea, I'll lose my mind. A big part of the trouble we have in the church today is that we have been content with mediocrity. We say, 'It doesn't matter as long as you are sincere.' But it does — and when we act like the church is somebody else's problem, what we get is a hodge-podge of teaching, preaching, attitudes, and aims." Even so, the church was still the place where all his thinking — all his lessons to me — ultimately came together in a continuing, dynamic conversation among Christians.

I don't think we can overlook the church as the ultimate source of many of the answers you and I are seeking. If Jesus Christ is real, then the church must also be real. It is Christ's church. He made it. It is his body. In a very literal way the church is Christ alive in the world. The person who says, "I don't care for the institutional church; I don't like the formality of it; and I don't like the bureaucracy of it," may be perfectly right. But that person also has to see that everything about the organization is not bad, and some great things get done through the bureaucracy and all those committees — services, gifts, programs that would not happen if a person were simply going it alone. Someone once declared that "Christianity which does not begin with the individual does not begin, but Christianity which ends with the individual simply ends." Not a bad point, do you think?

Truly, not a bad point at all. In my last two years of college, following my correspondence with my father and undoubtedly inspired by it, I researched and wrote my senior honors thesis on a contemporary topic in the sociology of religion. I chose to conduct the fieldwork for my study back home in Indianapolis, where family connections promised to lead me into productive territory. My particular topic was whether, and if so, how, the mainline churches — like the Presbyterian, Methodist, Lutheran, and Roman Catholic — had been affected by the political turmoil of the 1960s, including the churches' own frequent forays into those conflicts, especially in addressing the morality, or lack thereof, in the Vietnam War and the justice of the American civil rights movement. At the time of my study, each of those churches was steadily losing members, and at a statistically noteworthy rate. Meanwhile, the early 1970s also marked the beginning of a resurgence of Protestant fundamentalism and the rise of evangelical "new churches" in America. My assignment was to see if the decline of one and the growth of the other had a common origin in the engagements by the traditional, mainstream churches in social justice issues that had rocked the rest of America following the deaths of John and Robert Kennedy and Martin Luther King Jr.

To conduct my study, I had been given a fellowship by the John F. Kennedy Institute of Politics at Harvard University. This provided me a helpful platform from which to work. In the end, I chose to ask my research questions not through a wide sampling of public and parishioner opinion, but by intensive interviews and immersion in a single congregation. This allowed me to assemble a portrait of how at least one mainline church was faring as the social gospel of the 1960s drew to its inevitable and complicated close. With generous introductions from my father, I was invited to spend the summer interviewing members of a large, near-suburban Methodist church on the north side of Indianapolis. For the next three months, and within the limits of being a Presbyterian preacher's kid, I proceeded to become a part of this Methodist church family. I conducted over eighty interviews in parishioners' homes, asking them (usually in endless detail) why they did, or in some cases no longer did, attend church every Sunday morning. How could over a thousand busy, sophisticated, and thoughtful people — with so many options for their time and allegiance — regularly continue to choose the traditional church as a place to devote a valuable portion of their weekly time and, for many, considerably more of their resources and energies?

Their answers were diverse. Most said they belonged to a congregation, and attended church services, because they needed a place that offered a true perspective on their lives, a context for making the many choices that modern life seems to require on a daily, or even more frequent, basis. For them, the church offered a unique place where learning, reflection, and conversation about "what matters" were not only possible, but also expected. As one woman said to me at the time, "That church offers me a retelling of a way of living that I've never found anywhere else. If I didn't have the church and the standards of the church to judge life by, I would know a whole lot less about who I am or where I'm going. It gives me an idea of what I need to live up to, and why I should. Even though I don't go every Sunday, and when I do I don't know everyone there — far from it — it's my place. When I meet someone at work or at the mall and find out they're a member of my church too, I feel, oh boy, here's someone I can count on, one of my kind, and I feel better about my own beliefs."

These interviews took place a long time ago. Yet I suspect that were I to embark upon a similar project today, I would find many of the same sentiments about the church providing a context and a community for life's choices, a place to go to get a shared message about who and what matters. And I imagine I would hear even more about the value of the community of other Christians, in an age of virtual communication, "home commuting," and online conferences. In the same way that an in-person meeting conveys something that is simply missing from a conference call, a webcast, or an Internet exchange, the church offers a physical, communal reaffirmation of the "body of Christ" that has, at least for me, become all the more important as such experiences become rarer elsewhere. Communication so often seems to go hand in hand with isolation at a time when, if my daughter and her friends are representative examples, we often choose to text rather than talk even by the very cell phones designed to advance direct conversation. Church provides a real community, a facilitated conversation on values, a place to reflect and compare. It offers something of an antidote to what the sociologist Philip Rieff, in his 1966 study *The Triumph of the Therapeutic: Uses of Faith after Freud,* foresaw as "this culture, which once imagined itself inside a church, [and now] feels trapped in something like a zoo of separate cages."

Or does it? The title of Rieff's book suggests one direction the church has taken over the past thirty-five or forty years that arguably (and ironically) can lead people farther away from the "community of believers" and farther down a surprisingly conventional road of individual seeking for self-definition and fulfillment. I worry that this vision of the church as a center for finding individual healing and realizing personal identities may be yet another regrettable signature of my intensely self-focused generation of baby boomers. If so, it would be similar to our impact on so many other aspects of modern life.

Certainly, when I go back and look at my college thesis research, I see homegrown seeds of this "therapeutic Christianity" attempting to take root in the words of many I interviewed. For example, when I asked one member why she attended church services every Sunday morning, she remarked, "The church gives me a certain stability, something to cling to. I need it. I need something to hang on to when things are not going right. I want a hand to grasp out." Similarly, another member explained to me the real reasons he went to church: "All through the prior week, I have been faced with the problems of my life, and just life in general — social, economic, business, politics. On Sunday, I want to be reassured that life — or at least, my life — is going to be all right and that these are problems of the day where answers can be found in Christ's words. This gives me the reassurance that, on Monday, I can face life anew; on Monday, I can start fitting the example of Christ's life and his teachings that I'm going to have all through the next week."

My father and I never directly corresponded on this topic of the church as a private and personal refuge. But, always ahead of the curve, he did worry about a growing trend of Christian pursuit that too often emphasized the vision of Christ the healer in ways that obscured the authority of God the Father: "I'm disturbed, because I have suddenly come to realize that the church today lacks authority. We have been preaching sweetness and light and the heresy that all roads lead to God, when as a matter of fact we should have been speaking out on the demands of God and what real theology is all about."

Interesting to me, Colin Hansen, a writer on one of the emerging trends of twenty-first-century Christian thinking, so-called New Calvinism (new in the sense that the return of anything five hundred years old looks downright revolutionary), offers much the same observation that my father made over thirty-five years ago. As Hansen writes in his 2008 book *Young, Restless, Reformed: A Journalist's Journey with the New Calvinists:*

> Many churches geared toward so-called spiritual seekers focus on God's immanence, his nearness. They talk about a personal relationship with Christ, emphasizing his friendship and reminding audiences that God made us in his image. It all makes sense, because so many baby boomers left churches that felt impersonal and irrelevant. But the culture has shifted. Fewer Americans now claim any church background. Evangelical megachurches, once the upstart challengers, have become the new mainstream. Teenagers who grew up with buddy Jesus in youth group don't know as much about Father God.

What is it, then, as a twenty-first-century Christian, that makes me decide to get out of bed (or leave morning television) and turn out for Sunday worship, to support the church financially, to participate as an active member when there are so many other demands, from many other worthy organizations, on my time? Why do I "need" the church as a regular part of my own life?

I'm not sure my father (or for that matter, my grandfather, great-grandfather, or any of my other Presbyterian clergy forebears) would especially value my response to this question, or even consider it very coherent. Certainly, I don't share the same reverence for the church that any of them did. I will confess that I do not find its role in the world to be unique, as my father often suggested. Indeed, I have been involved with many community and social service agencies, over the course of my career, that I thought did a better or more effective job of carrying out a particular mission, or serving the needs of a particular population, than have the mission programs of large, denominational churches I have seen. But several factors still keep me showing up (even if not every Sunday morning) and make me want to remain on the membership rolls of a church congregation today.

To start with, at least for me, the church remains the only place where I can have an open conversation with others about faith, and learn more about my own through the message of good pastoral preaching. In my adult life, I have now belonged to several congregations (all Presbyterian, of course). I have observed, and undoubtedly, to some small extent, contributed to, the success of each through reasonably faithful attendance, regular church offering contributions, and, in one case, active participation in lay governance. Each congregation has had its own, distinctive personality. And some experiences have been far better than others. But overall, the churches that have lasted the longest and succeeded the best have been those whose pastors provided predictable, strong leadership and an especially strong, intellectually engaging Sunday morning message.

For the most part, Protestants of all types come not to participate in a ceremony but to hear, learn, reflect, and discuss. If the pastor does not provide the substance to get that conversation started, the congregation will not remain intact for very long. This lesson was especially clear to me in one congregation I belonged to, several years ago, whose senior pastor had been well liked but not loved, and who had proven himself capable of delivering sermons that were sometimes entertaining and occasionally erudite, but (if we are honest) rarely interesting. Church membership steadily declined, contributions dropped, and the congregation's best years seemed to be rooted firmly in the past. And then, following some difficult and even tragic developments, a new pastor arrived who insisted on engaging the congregation, on determining and delivering a message — often provocative — that would spark conversation to the point of debate. This new pastor had his own challenges. At the end of his relatively short tenure, he was not especially popular and, in truth, probably no better "loved" than his predecessor. But his edgy and pointed preaching restored the spark to the congregation; he provided the focal point for Sunday morning worship and discussion; and the church began to grow again.

There is a second set of reasons for church attendance — and in fact, these points should truly be first. They come down to this: if we are believers in the relevance of Christ's teachings, then we should probably take pretty seriously his directives to Peter and the apostles to "build my church" (Matt. 16:18). They, in fact, did — and many died for it. We should similarly pay attention to the mission of Paul in the early congregations throughout the ancient world proclaiming that Christ is indeed "the head of the body, the church" (Col. 1:18). From the start, we're supposed to understand that Christ's legacy is not only eternal but also, in a very real sense, institutional. Our belief is designed, and mandated, to be wrapped up in our belonging.

My father made a similar observation when he wrote to me about the importance of this continuing "body of Christ." He explained it in terms that mean even more to me today than when he originally wrote them:

> When Jesus was physically here in the body, he healed and comforted and taught and preached. He did all these things personally. Now Jesus is no longer physically present. So he has given the world his new body in a different form — the church. And a body — any body — must be organized or it can never function. So the real work of the church is to get organized and be obedient to the head, which is Christ. The real work of the church is to do the same work that Jesus did when he was physically present — ministering to others, being compassionate, healing, preaching, teaching. I think this is precisely how Jesus planned to make his impact on the world — through people, organized to present his message and do his work.

We live in an era when, as never before, many of our traditional institutions seem to be under heavy scrutiny and constantly in disrepair. I work closely with several large institutions in my own job every day — governments, large corporations, major research universities, social service organizations. I see what kind of stress is being brought to bear on all of them. Indeed, a big part of our own organization's mission is, from an economic development standpoint, to paint and then advance a compelling picture of an economic future where there are fewer large, traditional institutional employers and more small businesses, entrepreneurs, and start-up ventures on the landscape. That future can surely be exciting, but the change driving it is both disruptive and disturbing. Whether it is federal or state government, traditional political parties, or even large established companies and universities, most of our "organizational legacies" in this era are facing constant questioning, are equally mistrusted, seem constantly to be "reinventing" themselves, and are often threatened with sudden extinction by the powers of modern communication and the forces of global markets.

The church is one of these institutions under siege, although in the church's case, siege is not a new state. The church's existence has been challenged from the start. It has splintered, separated, purged, reformed, reunited, factionalized, merged, grown, atrophied, and been reborn in the course of spreading to every continent except Antarctica over nearly two thousand years. I heard a history lecture recently that described the Roman army as one of the oldest institutions in the world; but of course, the Roman army of Christ's day — or Constantine's — has long since ceased to exist. The church has been there throughout. It has changed history, and it has itself changed over the course of history. It has gotten caught up in an astounding range of political and social issues and causes, often to its detriment. It has done a great deal of good, and caused a great deal of harm and suffering in the name of Christ throughout the world. But its mission remains: recognizable, always controversial, still a central part of life's story.

I'm a creature of institutions. I know of no other institution like this. In a world and at a time where everything seems constantly new, this is something old and remarkably constant to which anyone claiming to be a Christian had better be paying attention — and in some way, participating.

Throughout our correspondence, my father stressed the unique mission and standing of the church, even as he readily acknowledged its many accumulated faults. These eloquent sentences capture his feelings well:

I know a great many more things that are wrong with the church than does the average critic. I know it has often been blind and foolish, proud and stubborn. I know that what Robert Ingersoll is purported once to have said is true: that the church has been all too often willing to trade off treasures in heaven for cash down here. I know that the church has sponsored bloody persecutions throughout history, and I know that at times it has stayed the advancement of truth. The church has been brave, as it surely was during the civil rights movement of the 1960s, but it has much to make up for when it comes to social justice. In the past it has fostered a segregated society (both racially and culturally) in America. I know that the church has not always been responsive to the needs of the world, and I can believe that the judgment of God may be on his church for its race and class consciousness, for its worldliness, for its sects and divisions.

I know all that; but I know other things too. Without the church and its message, you could not believe and think as you do. The church is really the only institution, the only agency, to bring people to an understanding of God. There are a lot of organizations for recreation, for study and fellowship, for moral uplift. But only the church speaks to the total person. Still today, the church that Christ founded continues to serve, continues to administer the life-affirming sacraments, continues to preach the gospel, continues to engage in good works. The church does what no other group on earth can or will do: it points to God — and even in its often poor way, it tries to work his will.

As noted earlier, I'm not at all sure my father was right when he so regularly found the church's role to be unique in every respect. Indeed, I believe there are several other institutions beyond the church that also, in their own ways and not always in explicit discipleship, carry out the will of God in the world. However, I very much agree with my father on one final, essential point: the church is just part of the package when it comes to any Christian's relationship with God. It's not optional; it's inseparable. Christianity at its heart is not an individual, soul-searching, or soul-saving pursuit; Christ's whole point was to create a community of believers who are individually important but whose corporate existence is also supposed to work as something valuable in and of itself. The church is not a venue for our entertainment, a show that we can take in or ignore as we choose. If we put our faith in the authority of God and the love of Christ, then the church not only comes with the territory — it is the territory. And if the church isn't measuring up to its goals (which, of course, it fails to do on a regular basis), then it is our institution, our problem to fix.

Despite all the obstacles and the constant predictions for its demise, I strongly suspect the church will continue on. But new challenges present themselves. Recent public opinion polling of the current "millennial" generation of young Americans (those born from 1981 to 2000) shows a group of young adults far different from my group in many ways. Many of those differences (including reportedly greater tolerance for and less suspicion of people my age) are good. Indeed, this appears to be a new generation less hostile to parental authority but more open to change and considerably more tolerant of difference in race, gender, and sexual orientation. It also seems to be interested in religion and spirituality. But far more than any group on record, this is a cohort of young Americans that in significant numbers — more than 25 percent, according to a recent Pew survey — declares itself unaffiliated with any particular religious faith. Data from previous generations give reassurance that, as we age, we tend to pay more attention to matters of religious belief. Where we start in this journey, however, is significant, and can set the patterns for lifetimes and the demographic trends for decades. For this generation, the competition for attention and devotion is likely to be fierce.

Perhaps this time, for the church to continue to thrive, it will take even more help. Certainly, there's a personal message here for me, since my own daughter is a member of this generation on the ascendant. I need to be paying attention. Here again, as my father would no doubt remind me, for those of us who call ourselves Christians, it's past time to get to work.

The Eighth Lesson

THE NEED FOR A GOOD WITNESS

A few years ago, when my wife and I became official members of our current congregation, we were required to take several weeks of "explorer" classes explaining what the church did, how it addressed the world through preaching and mission, and the various ways members could participate. I will confess to being annoyed, at first, with this requirement for submission to such instruction, believing yet again that, somehow, my credentials as a preacher's kid (and a Presbyterian one, at that) should give me the equivalent of a lifetime passport into any congregation I might choose to join.

Still, we took the classes. They were well taught, and of course had the added benefit of putting us in closer and better fellowship with both the pastoral staff and our fellow parishioners. Three weeks into the exercise, my wife and I had to acknowledge that we were actually enjoying the experience, and learning quite a bit from it. Ten weeks in, we "graduated," and on one Sunday morning we found ourselves as part of a group of some eighty-five new members formally recognized and welcomed into the church during a Sunday morning service. Part of our welcoming ceremony involved a public reaffirmation of our beliefs in response to questions posed by the senior pastor. As I recall, there were six questions, progressively seeking our affirmation that we believed solely in the God of Christ; that we would open our hearts to transformation by God's word, as recounted in the New Testament; that we would endeavor to embrace the world, and others in it, with "arms of love"; that we would humble ourselves before God in prayer; that we recognized our duty to participate in a Christian community of service and stewardship; and that we would actively participate as members of the church in developing 10,000 new disciples and partnering with other churches to create 150 new congregations around the globe within the next ten years.

As peculiar as this may sound, I have always enjoyed the strong sense of belonging that stirs within me when I participate in spoken affirmations, whether of patriotism or religious faith. Something happens to words when they are uttered publicly, in the company and with the joined voices of others, that makes them far more compelling and, certainly, more powerful. These are moments in which we feel, through shared and careful speech, that we are after all part of something larger than ourselves. In my congregational vows, I readily responded in the affirmative with either a hearty "Yes" or an enthusiastic "I do" to the first five of those six questions. Casting aside any doubts, fears, nuances, or quibbling I might have had over the wording of a question, I found myself publicly affirming my fidelity to God; to the Christ of the New Testament; to love and humility; to the power of prayer; and to the necessity and nobility of Christian service.

But on that sixth question — the one about bringing others to Christ, spreading the gospel in the world, and building new congregations — I really, really hesitated. That just isn't me, said a nagging voice in my head; evangelism makes my skin crawl. I don't want to be like one of those people that goes door to door, earnestly "selling" the good news. I thought of other things I disliked doing intensely — say, raising money for various causes and campaigns — and knew that in a heartbeat, I'd choose asking someone to contribute five thousand dollars to some dismal political candidate I couldn't possibly like, over suggesting to that same person that he or she talk to me about forming a relationship of faith with a God I profess to love. It was a very bad, and a very long, moment. Finally, because scores of other eager Christians were standing alongside me waiting their turn to affirm these questions, I did muster a "yes, I will." But it was truly a still, small voice. I knew — and so did anyone else who was listening — that on question number six, the one about evangelism, my heart just wasn't in it.

Why is evangelism so hard for Christians? After all, it's what Christ told us to do. It's how the church has grown to what it is, and where it is, today. It's what Christians have lived for, and died for, over more than two millennia. And it is indeed about sharing the gospel, the "good news." As human beings, we're practically hardwired to run and tell a friend, neighbor, or partner the moment something good, or something bad, happens to us (and when it's bad and happens to someone else, it readily distills into gossip, which we joyously love to spread even more). Life's events really are meant to be observed through sharing. Hence, I'm puzzled that sharing the good news of Christianity seems so awkward.

My father and I didn't really correspond on this particular topic, but over the years since that correspondence, I've considered several possible reasons for my shyness in the field of Christian communications. First, I've conjectured, perhaps it's all just too complex to summarize very easily, or very well. After all, I've had the advantage of my father's basic lessons for nearly forty years now, and I'm still putting my beliefs together. How could I possibly be prepared to tell this story to others?

But then, when I'm honest about it, I recognize that in other fields, I've somehow managed to find workable ways to get my point across, even when that point is fairly complicated.

I think back to my political campaign, for example. As a candidate, I developed my skills to the point that I could deliver the main rationales for my candidacy in well under a minute. Speed was, of course, important there, because a minute often exceeded the amount of time I was likely to be granted by someone silent (and often pretty sullen) on the receiving end of a very cold, political fund-raising call. To this day, I can still skate across the talking points of the four best ways to reduce the federal budget deficit, or the importance of voting as the best way to ensure that our state or city remains the "best place to live, work, and raise a family." Short messages on big topics often succeed in televised, thirty-second political advertisements as well. Thirty seconds may sound like a brief time in which to deliver a decent message, but I learned as a candidate (and now appreciate even more as a viewer) that most candidates can say all that's really needed, or at least all that anyone really wants to hear, in well under a half-minute, and still have leftover time to smile, shoot a basketball (or a gun), or hug a spouse. A commercial lasting a minute is a "documentary"; the prospect of enduring a political message extending three or even five minutes is simply too painful to contemplate.

Similarly, when it comes to explaining a complex subject and mission, I also think about what companies manage to do every instant of every day with targeted and focused messages on television, radio, and the Internet: they tell what they hope will be a compelling and pertinent part of a much larger and far more complicated story. I consider what I'm doing for a living now. The organization I run involves lots of public and private parties who have managed to come together and invest in a unique enterprise. Over the past five years, this organization has raised nearly a quarter of a billion dollars for a wide variety of purposes. It invests in new companies. It assists state and local government in attracting and building other new businesses. It carries out research, and publishes expert reports. It has started a health information network to link hospitals, clinics, physicians, and patients electronically for that long-awaited "future of health care." It has organized an online network of young professionals, sponsored numerous science fairs, and led the charge for better science and math education for our children. It holds conferences, buys dinners, and hands out awards.

Explaining all this at once to any audience is a large and

confusing and, generally, unnecessary task. It's unnecessary because different groups are interested in different parts of the story. Investors care about the companies. Parents and educators care about the programs for high school algebra. University officials care about technology transfer. So the message ends up starting with what a particular person, or group, cares about. It then seeks to convey responsive information to that specific interest and, also, the more general impression that beyond the particular question, there is something larger and more engaging, an organization perhaps worth learning more about and visiting again. Ours is an inherently "fuzzy" brand, yielding a messy message. Yet, it works.

So why can't I employ a similar strategy when it comes to discussing Christianity?

Perhaps on questions of faith, it is just more difficult to know where to begin, and almost impossible to know when and where to end once the discussion gets going. Religion, after all, is a subject literally as complex as life itself. Very few people we know — and probably, almost no one we have just met — are likely to give us the time to get an evangelistic message out in a way that feels, at least to us, genuine, personal, and complete.

Still, if I'm at all honest on this topic, such a "complexity" argument sounds mighty lame. After all, the whole point of the Gospels, the letters and the teachings and the touring of Paul, and more than two thousand years of the mission of the church is that the story of Christ is at last supposed to represent a message from God in understandable, human form that must — and can — be told. We may not be able to get all the details right. We may argue over what a parable meant, or whether some reported miracle was literally true. But after being privileged to view the wider canvas, we ought to be able to scratch out at least a few line drawings, or take a few broad brushstrokes, to convey some of what we see to others.

The complexity argument is even less valid when we acknowledge that it is fully acceptable, in telling any story of value, to start somewhere specific without unloading all the details at once. In fact, it's a fundamental part of any story: a good one takes time to tell. Religion seems to make us unduly anxious, and we fret that we need to get the entire message out all at once. But eventually, we can master our fears and insecurities and get on with it. My father drew on his own, very personal experience to make just this point in one of his early letters to me:

As you will probably recall, my very first pastoral call was a joint appointment to the small, neighboring Salem and Zion churches near Venedocia, Ohio. Most of my parishioners in these two congregations were of proud Welsh Presbyterian descent, and I was called as the first minister in their 100-year history who did not speak Welsh. I had just graduated from seminary, and was recently engaged to be married to your mother — so the stakes for me were very high when I ascended the pulpit at Salem church, for the first time in my life, and gave my inaugural sermon to those stern-looking elders sitting in the front pews. The sermon lasted just twelve minutes. In it I tried to be sure that I said *everything* I knew about God, the church, the Bible, religion, and life. When I was through,

I retired to the loneliness of my study. Only then did I consider the situation: I had just told my congregation everything I believed to be true. I had nothing more to say to them. What was I to do next week? More to the point, what was I to do for the next forty-plus years?

He did the math, and the situation appeared to grow even worse:

I sat down and figured that here I was, twenty-three years old and with one sermon done. If I were to preach until I was sixty-five, that would mean forty-two years of sermons. At the rate of fifty per year, that would mean I had to write and preach twenty-one hundred separate sermons — and here I was, done in with one! Gradually, I came to my senses and learned to take these challenges one step at a time. I didn't have to cover the whole Bible in one sermon — I just had to concentrate on a single text, a single idea. Week by week, Sunday by Sunday, I had to think, focus, and then express myself, concept by concept, message by message. That's how we succeed at communicating anything as human beings — including religion. Nothing — and especially nothing wondrously complex and vital — can be summed up in a single conversation or through a single letter. So I learned, and hope you will learn, that you do indeed have to start somewhere; but you don't have to arrive everywhere all at once.

If complexity is not a valid excuse for failing to spread the good news of the Gospels, then perhaps the awkwardness stems from the fact that the message itself has become a franchise damaged beyond repair by its previous messengers. For too long, too many have tried to peddle religious belief like some curbside commodity, or as a pretext to trade or prey upon fragile human emotions in cynical efforts to corral converts or raise cash.

This sorry story is not just one of sordid individual conduct, either; the church itself has a long and tarnished record when it comes to institutional evangelism. The spreading of the "good news" to Central and South America in the fifteenth and sixteenth centuries, for example, quickly led to the brutal elimination of multiple indigenous cultures by so-called Christian conquerors from Spain. For well over a thousand years, a succession of wars, large and small, has righteously condoned widespread and often indiscriminate killing in the name of Christ. When it comes to the history of the Christian church, there are so many examples of breaking faith that it is difficult even to know where to begin to catalogue them.

But I can think of other institutions, and messages, considerably less worthy — and far more unsavory — where many of us are still somehow willing to stand up and be counted. Once again, take politics. For that matter, take political fundraising, a subject I know all too well. Now here's an example of a truly "damaged franchise." Political campaigning is a field of endeavor richly endowed with hallmark attributes of pandering to special interests, building messages and whole candidacies around false fears, misguided hopes, and other assorted distortions of the truth. Yet we have all seen examples of political campaigns, from both major political parties and on all levels, that managed to produce messages and messengers that could stir genuine enthusiasm and hope, at least among some voters. And those voters responded by giving their time and their money to the cause.

Cynics insist that such people usually participate in the political process out of wholly secular and extremely selfish interests. Road contractors contribute in anticipation of lucrative contracts some day; trial lawyers give in hopes that the candidate, if elected, will block litigation reform; insurance companies give because they are, apparently, even more unpopular than the politicians asking for support and thus need all the allies they can find. Those cynics may capture a part of the truth, as they often do. Yet the picture they paint is not true to many campaign experiences, including my own.

From the beginning, mine was a campaign where everyone I saw, called, wrote, or otherwise pestered knew beyond a doubt that I was going to lose — the only question being by how much. I remember when an older supporter of mine, who helped me raise considerable funds, showed up in my campaign office one day wearing a T-shirt with what he said was a special message just for me: "BELIEVE." This extraordinarily kind soul was saying he was prepared to stick with me, despite the long odds, if I truly believed I could win and could convince others like him.

It was good advice for politics — and for life. And I acted on it. Although I didn't personally know most of those I asked for support, I knew from their prior campaign giving histories (all readily available online) that I was making my cold calls on people who were generally prepared to support passionate candidates, even in long-shot efforts, because they cared so much about making some sort of political change. Silly as I was to indulge in such fantasy, I really did manage to believe, when I engaged these fund-raising and campaign prospects, that I could win, that I would win, and that winning would make a difference. I proceeded to tell them why, in ways and undoubtedly with a level of enthusiasm that might have made them doubt my IQ, but usually did not lead them to mistrust my motives. Many (in truth, most) still politely said, "No, thanks." But more than a few said, "OK."

And through it all, somehow, I managed to overcome shyness, cynicism, disbelief, and even, in a sense, reason to make my case. It was the toughest thing I have ever done, or most likely, will ever attempt to do. But from this experience I learned the valuable lesson that even a dead-sure loser can raise over a million dollars when people believe he's putting his heart and soul into it.

So again, for me the question becomes: If my faith is as important to me as I have claimed over a lifetime of discussions, letters, church services, and so many other actions — then why can't I try to bring others to it, at least with the same level of effort that I sought to bring friendly doubters to a laughably long-shot political campaign?

Maybe the truth is far simpler: perhaps our beliefs are simply too close for comfort when it comes to telling others. After all, questions of faith are, for most people, even more fundamental, more personal, than questions of political preferences or social issues. In a different way but with the same result, opening a conversation on religious belief feels like discussing the most intimate topics of sex or revealing our deepest and darkest secrets to strangers. If we're normal, awake, and lucid, we simply are inclined to discuss anything but such a topic.

The flip side of the preceding sentence is also true: if we appear to be too eager to discuss our religious views, then there's a fair chance that people may think less of us because of it. I, for one, just don't want to be opening up a line of discussion when the person sitting across the table from me, no matter how intently or sincerely focused he or she may seem on my remarks, might be secretly thinking, "Uh-oh, and just where is this guy going?"

We all have experiences with others seeking to intrude into our lives or conversations, bringing unwanted affirmations of faith. Too often, these seem to be the very types of individuals we would most like to avoid — not just as messengers, but as people. As my father observed:

Some old saint long ago said that we Christians ought to be like "little Christs." It's a pretty good phrase, but, unfortunately, too many of us have had experiences that lead us to associate this kind of Christian sincerity with an unhealthy overdose of strangeness. One member of my congregation told me recently, and with some measure of concern, about her cousin who had decided to go out and help organize a new church of charismatic followers. She said this cousin has been "on high" ever since she started this project, and that she seems to be becoming a "little weird." God's love in our life shouldn't make us weird — not even remotely so. Good theology ought to make us more compelling as people, more warm and genuine and credible, I think.

Yet here again, explaining my evangelical shyness by describing my faith as either too close or too "hot" a topic for me to bring out in normal conversation seems far too convenient. In the past, I have tried to assuage my guilt on this point by telling myself that my alternative to bringing up questions of faith will be to set the stage for others to ask me about them. In this fantasy, my exemplary virtue will shine through so brightly that the day will come, and the moment in the conversation will arise, when someone will just be moved to say, "So, why are you like this?" Of course, that day never really comes; people don't customarily come to sudden realizations through some series of subtle clues. Even more to the point, how often does someone do any of us the favor of asking us to describe, in glorious detail, all the many reasons that we are as wonderful as we know we truly are? This response of "too personal; too strange — so just wait for the right opportunity" is probably the weakest of all.

Just because many people fail to discuss faith in a credible or welcome way with others doesn't mean we get a pass from doing it. There are all kinds of topics I would rather not discuss, and all sorts of conversations, at work and at home, that are painful, personal, and overall wonderful prospects for avoidance. I may not handle discussions on any of these topics especially well, and I may need to have them more than once to get my point across. But really, and especially in today's world, can there be conversations on subjects so important that they are effectively off-limits?

When I was growing up, I was taught by my parents that it was best, at least in "polite company" (whatever that actually was), to avoid any mention of politics or religion. Unstated, but also pretty much off the table, were discussions about racial issues, equal opportunity for women in employment, or gender preferences (the very concept was so novel that no one had thought to ban it in the first place). We are, thankfully, a long way from those times, and all these topics and many more are the subjects not only of conversations but also of constant cable news presentations, movies, books, and Internet blogs. We live in an era when open communication on virtually any topic is championed. Discussions of faith shouldn't be relegated to a whole separate universe.

Indeed, I see frequent examples of people who manage to present their religious perspective to others without seeming forced, vulnerable, or strange.

I think of one of my scientific colleagues who, last year, enclosed with his Christmas card a separate note on seeing the miracle of Christmas through the eyes of his youngest child. It was a lovely sentiment, and made me aware of a dimension to his personality that I found not strange at all, but encouraging and affirming. That note has in fact given me the courage, from time to time, to venture with this person into discussions of religion, along with the many other topics we discuss.

I think of one of my daughter's lifelong friends. Her parents, immigrants from Pakistan, encouraged her, upon entering adolescence, to conform to Muslim tradition and observe all the formalities of her faith, including the wearing of the *hijab,* the traditional head covering for Muslim women. This is an open, bright, and enthusiastic girl, with strong social skills and many friends. The decision to (somewhat literally) set herself apart from her peers in this way could not have been an easy one. She is one of the few Muslims attending a Jesuit high school, located in the comparatively conservative midwestern United States, and at an age when most are seeking to fit in rather than to stand out from others. Moreover, we live in an era when neither the general symbols of the Muslim faith nor the specific reminders of the traditional role of women in Muslim society are easily acceptable in many parts of American culture.

Yet somehow, this young woman pulls the whole thing together. When she's around our house, I have no concern that she will suddenly start some awkward discussion of religious differences (indeed, we have had her share Christmas Eve dinner with us more than once, since she is such a delightful and such a reliable guest). But I have no doubt at all that if I asked her about her beliefs, she could give me a succinct and convincing presentation of her Muslim faith.

I think of another young woman, further along in life, who asked me to meet with her recently for career advice. Trained as a lawyer, this is someone who had been working in a senior management position, looking to make a change in professional direction as she and her husband work together to puzzle through the logistical challenges of dual-career families with young children. We discussed a variety of options and also the many ways that people process information and make decisions, including through social networks, web-based research, formal career counseling, and discussions with friends and family. At one point toward the end of the conversation she observed, "I am going through this process every day now, and I think I'm making progress. Certainly, I have a lot to consider each night when I pray before I go to bed." Our conversation neither stopped nor started to turn toward religion at that point. After she made this remark, I had no different view of her sincerity, her focus, or her approach to the very practical problems she was seeking to sort through. Yet she had told me something about herself that was important, without seeming in the least bit strange. She had acknowledged the Christian context for her in making significant life choices. Feeling that familiar discomfort, I had remained silent on the entire subject. At the end of our conversation, I realized that, somehow, while I certainly had more to say that day about career options, she ended up with the better statement about what matters most in life.

And so I come back to that sixth vow to my church congregation. I am not sure if I will ever be ready to commit to going out and helping to build 150 new churches, or finding 10,000 new Christians to attend them. I'm not even sure if that's an appropriate mission. But I am sure I believe something, and that what I believe is important. I have a relationship of faith worth talking about, one that's worthy of telling to others, in a way that's credible to me. As my third-grade teacher once counseled, I need to overcome my boyhood shyness and start speaking up more. Maybe if I do, I just might get better at it.

The Last Word

FIRST STEPS, ENDLESS LESSONS

❧

W

hen I was growing up, I used to wonder why all churches, including ours, featured events so focused on coffee. Men's prayer breakfasts, church dinners, morning Bible studies, and, of course, the very concept of that Sunday morning staple, the intraservice "coffee hour" itself, all revolved around the consumption of large quantities of generally mediocre-quality versions of this beverage, brewed by volume discount in the service of larger stewardship.

Looking back on all this, I now think the church put its finger on something smart (Howard Schultz and the folks that founded Starbucks also figured this out really well). Many great conversations do in fact take place around events where neither wine nor beer nor champagne but simple coffee — often accompanied by food — plays a prominent role.

To demonstrate the truth of this statement, I think of my own professional history. There were my first recruiting lunches with law firms, where the hiring pitches for employment came as coffee was served at the end of what was, typically, the most expensive meal I had enjoyed in months. There was what turned out to be my actual job interview for my first job out of law school, as a junior staff member for the U.S. Senate Foreign Relations Committee. The interview took place when I observed the chief of staff to the committee chairman having lunch in his office, and I had both the temerity and the resourcefulness to bring up a couple cups of coffee from the Senate cafeteria as my offering and, as it turned out, opening to a very productive conversation. (I had been bothering this guy for an interview for months, and once he saw the coffee, he just decided to get it over with.) And then there was the series of breakfast meetings — again, with coffee in prominent attendance — that convinced me to take my current position. In that role today, I often get calls from people I don't know very well, volunteering to buy me "a cup of coffee." Such a request is always code for a plea for help in strategizing or networking for a next career move.

Coffee conversations are simply more significant, and more appropriately intimate, than office visits. Coffee gives us standing to introduce serious, often personal topics without the distractions of a larger meal. Coffee provides a smooth transition through some of life's most difficult moments. Churches may have missed the boat in addressing some of history's greatest events. But when it comes to coffee, they seem to get it right.

Now that I'm thinking more seriously about discussions with others on the topic of belief (I'm still shying away from calling this anything like "evangelism"), I should probably be thinking more about coffee. I consider what it would be like to be sitting at breakfast, sometime soon, with a pot between me and my guest, as he or she and I discuss various important topics of the day. For some reason on this still-imaginary morning, the conversation suddenly becomes more serious. Perhaps one of us mentions a common friend facing a midlife career crisis. Maybe some mutual colleague stops by the table and mentions his teenaged son's serious illness. Whatever the cause, we are now moving to questions of values, social concerns, or personal growth. I sense that my opening is coming.

And then my guest hands it to me. She or he says something along the lines of, "You seem to have thought a lot about this issue, and feel strongly about it. What sort of beliefs do you have that make you care about this so much?"

Here is of course that long-awaited, long-odds moment when it is not my courage but another's curiosity that coaxes me into discussing my approach to life's great issues of faith.

OK, this moment may never come. It probably won't. But it might. What would I say?

First, I hope I would have enough sense — and grace — to pause and consider the person asking the question. Who is it? How well do I know her, and what she values? What does he likely think of me? Is there any sense in which I am viewed by this person, on any topic at all, as someone entitled to have an opinion, someone who is a trustworthy authority? The answers to those questions would all, of course, need to come to me instantly, and would determine where I start. Assuming a conclusion that I might be heard, I think I'd try to say a great deal. I'd start by deliberately calling myself out as a Christian. I would of course note my family background, my many forebears who were seminarians, the extraordinary person and example of my father.

My father — I'd talk a lot about him and, I suspect, try to borrow a bit of his credibility on these topics. I would acknowledge that, forty years after our initial family conversations, Christianity still makes sense to me, more than any other way I can look at the portion of the world we know, as well as the far greater portion we don't. I'd observe that an underlying belief in a God-created universe, one that knows us each and designed us all, has turned out to stand the test of intervening years pretty well for me. Very quickly, though, I would need to acknowledge that life has also, and in many ways, been extremely good to me, whether in marriage, in fatherhood, or in profession. Certainly, there have been real disappointments. Yet at least so far, I have undoubtedly had far less than my theoretically fair share of genuine sorrow or suffering. Put a slightly different way, I seem to have been spared most of those crises of fate that put many people's belief in God — or at least, their conviction that God is concerned about them — to the test.

Acknowledging my life's important lack of drama, I'd then talk briefly about my own journey over that time, and my views of human selfishness, the real power of evil, and the miracle that God still seems to care about us. This is all pretty heavy lifting, of course, and my proclivities toward excessive earnestness would truly be put to the test here.

I would try to move on to focus (a great deal, I think) on the benefits and burdens of living a life designed not only to fill up our time today, but also to establish a template of character and values with the beginnings of enough content to last an eternity. I would try to be realistic about how little anyone can know when it comes to the best ways to pursue such an objective, beyond seeking to be the best sort of person and connected, compassionate soul we can be. And I hope I would insist that we should nevertheless make this effort — not because it makes us "saved," but because it makes us more.

At this point, the conversation would undoubtedly be lagging. My questioner would probably be regretting ever asking me the starting question. Certainly, I'd be checking the pot for another cup of coffee.

Time to drink up, and wrap up. I'd quickly try to characterize sin not as a series of bad deeds, but as an overindulgence in selfishness. I'd apologize for the church while still, I hope, affirming its importance.

And I'd acknowledge the many things I just don't understand.

I would note that, rushing through middle age, what I find perhaps hardest to believe is that any of us could place so much faith in the infallibility of human knowledge or our understanding of the ways of the universe that we would ever presume we can judge whether God, Christ, or religion in general is "credible." Given our clear limits, any such childlike faith in man's ability to know seems naive in the extreme. If I ever referred to any Bible passage at all, this is the time I would recall the words of the apostle Paul in 1 Corinthians 13:12 — "For now we see in a mirror, dimly, but then we will see face to face. Now I know only in part; then I will know fully, even as I have been fully known." I would acknowledge getting considerably more accustomed to being nearsighted — in many ways.

If I really did get this far, then it would be time for this conversation to come to a close. I've always struggled with effective endings, and I'm far from sure how I can ever accomplish such a feat here. I'm drifting. I'm thinking of another conversation I wish I could have, with yet another person sitting before me, my own father and first teacher. This new conversation would not call for my response to someone else's questions of faith; it would command my silence as I listened to what I hope would be answers to my own.

Because there remains much to ask. And the truth is, there are still issues for me that just don't add up. Though operating from a position generally inside the tent of Christian belief, I have questions that really give me pause.

For example, even with an abiding belief in the possibility and potential of eternal life, shouldn't I, as a relatively well-off person in twenty-first-century America, be fairly distressed about Christ's observation (Matt. 19:24) to his disciples, "Again I tell you, it is easier for a camel to go through the eye of a needle than for someone who is rich to enter the kingdom of God"?

Or this: If Christians really are supposed to make an imperfect world into a better place, why then didn't Christ himself get more indignant and command his church to address the struggles of human poverty, instead of just making the seemingly offhand observation, "For you always have the poor with you, but you will not always have me" (Matt. 26:11)? How can Christ appear to be so fatalistic about a world that surely he could change, or direct others to improve?

And speaking of Christ, how will we know if he is coming again? Like my father, I am not inclined to the essentially immobilizing view of some large and loud and apocalyptic "second coming." Still, how should I be waiting for Christ in this world? How do I avoid the cluelessness of those debating apostles on the road to Emmaus, who in the early days following the crucifixion are so caught up in their theological dithering that they fail to recognize the risen Christ, walking right there alongside them? Certainly, this is a moment that could, and most likely will, never happen for me. Yet the promise of God's open-ended love in the New Testament must also make this a moment that could happen to any of us in the next five minutes. How could I possibly be ready? How can I ever be paying sufficient attention to life, to people, to events not to miss it?

I am unlikely to find answers to these or many other questions anytime soon. I need to work with what I have already been given.

I am, after all, fortunate to have been the early recipient of eight solid lessons on life, followed by a ninth lesson on the subject of death, from a father who had much to teach me. He showed me that life must indeed be lived with an edge, with intellect and ambition and attention relentlessly engaged over the rhythm of days and across the tumult of human relationships. He taught me not only how to see God, but how to listen for him — and how to wait. He so often exemplified for me what matters, who matters, how to act. Simply put, he personified love, and so made it credible for me to believe in a God who has personified love in Christ.

From these lessons I have been able to fashion a faith, a relationship with God and with others, that tells me pretty clearly how I am supposed to live, and the kinds of choices I am supposed to make. It's time for me to recognize that when it comes to faith, I am, at last, an adult. There will always be questions. But there are so many significant things to do, right here and now, that the questions just can't get in the way.

Perhaps I should consider ordering another pot of coffee. It's important to be fully awake. After all, it's impossible to know when and where I may yet have, or have again, the warm and gentle experience of God's unmistakable grace.